The SUNSET GRILL CHRONICLES

The
SUNSET
GRILL
CHRONICLES

PHILIP GOLABUK

Wynwood® Press
Tarrytown, New York

Grateful acknowledgment is made for permission to include the following: *p. 71,* from Michael Luciano Ventura, © 1990 by Michael L. Ventura; *p. 83,* from *Letters to a Young Poet* by Rainer Maria Rilke. Translation by M. D. Herter Norton. Copyright 1934 by W. W. Norton & Company, Inc. Renewed 1962 by M. D. Herter Norton. Revised edition copyright 1954 by W. W. Norton & Company. Reprinted by permission of the publisher; *p. 131,* from *Bananas* (Woody Allen), with permission of MGM Pathé; *p. 162,* from *Shadow Dancing in the U.S.A.* by Michael Ventura. Used with the author's permission; *p.164,* from "Peaceful Easy Feeling" (Jack Tempchin), © 1973 Jazz Bird Music & WB Music Corp. All Rights on Behalf of Jazz Bird. Music administered by WB Music Corp. All Rights Reserved. Used by permission.

Library of Congress Cataloging-in-Publication Data

Golabuk, Philip.
   [The] Sunset Grill Chronicles / Philip Golabuk. — 1st ed.
      p.   cm.
   ISBN 0-922066-78-7
   1. Love. 2. Friendship. 3. Courtship—Psychological aspects.
  4. Interpersonal relations. I. Title.
  BF575.L8G64   1992
  158'.2—dc20   91-28673
                                     CIP

Copyright © 1992 by Philip Golabuk
Published by Wynwood® Press
Tarrytown, New York
An Imprint of Gleneida Publishing Group
Printed in the United States of America
First Edition

To
Samara
with seven-course love

Contents

This above all: to thine own self be true . . .
—Shakespeare
Hamlet, Act I, sc.iii

Acknowledgments

We all want to get to the appetizer, main course, and dessert, so I'll make this brief. Acknowledgments go to Tim and Sonny, the owners of the Sunset Grill restaurant; to general manager Steve; to managers Sheryl, Coleman, and Brian, whose name is not Jeff; and to servers Brian, Stacey, Peter, Jeff, and Susan. Thank you all for the good food, the laughs, the great service, the willingness to lend your name and reputation to these pages, and for your endless patience while my friends and I tied up a table for hours sipping coffee and water with lemon wedges. I'm indebted to the members of the Sunset Grill society for their persistent courage, honesty, and willingness to take next steps—Kären, Dennis, Gretchen, and Rick, and additionally to Kären for giving this book its title and daring me to write it.

I want to acknowledge as honorary members of the Grill society, my sister, Linda; brother, Bob; sister-in-law, Donna Rhodes; and family tykes Jessica, Jeremy, and Jason; also my wonderful daughter, Samara; irrepressible parents, Mike and Mildred; and my friends and teachers Bubsey Levy, Norman

Hering, Beatrix Aldana, Dave Baker, Saviz and Maheen Shafaie, Daniel Salvano, Bob Miller, Jimi Millikan, and the late Tom Hanna. Special appreciation is extended to Linda Marais for her peerless style, wit, warmth, wisecracks, and unwavering faith in me and my work.

A final note of thanks goes to Robert Manley, president of Gleneida Publishing Group, for believing wholeheartedly in this book; to my editor, Patricia Kossmann; to Nancy Jillard and Marina Marketos for their excellent copyediting; to Marie Stilkind at Health Communications Incorporated; and to my literary agent, Elizabeth Frost Knappman of New England Publishing Associates. Every book is a collaboration of the influences and energies of many, and had I attempted this one without the confidence, encouragement, and talent of these people, you would not be reading it.

Preface

This is a book about <u>love</u>. Its four sections are arranged developmentally as a kind of map of the evolution several of us went through on our way to learning a little about what love is and isn't. There are no prescriptions, no answers in these chronicles, except where I may have got carried away. Instead, you'll find a candid sharing of the questions we faced and what we saw when we faced them—not academic or theoretical questions, but questions that, served up by heartbreak and other crises of the soul, often held us by the throat and refused to let go until we did face them.

Maybe we chose a restaurant for our meeting place because we were hungry—for life, for respite from the worst in us, for a second or third or fourth chance after too many years spent wandering in the circles of our own unawareness and blundering. Having passed undeniably into mid-life, some of us realized that we were in danger of becoming cynical about love. So much goes by the word nowadays. As children of the sixties, we'd seen love in its heyday, when it was "free." But the legacy of those intensely experimental years, followed by a certain relative flatness and loss of zeitgeist in the two decades that followed, had left us with much confusion and not much with which to rebuild. As it turned out, we weren't just hungry. We were starving. And what we found in each other, at the Grill, fed us and gave us back the strength of spirit that tells you that being alive is a good deal and not just some stupid, pointless exercise in disappointment and worry.

The actual meat-and-potatoes portion of the *Chronicles* begins with a section called "Hardship" because it was the tough times that brought us together at the Grill. Here, you'll find candid observations on faith, knowing and not knowing, antidepressants, losing and finding the things that matter, and what's really going on behind the scenes of so-called men's and women's issues. From this starting point, we move on to the next section, "Friendship," as the members of the Grill society did, discovering that, although each of us has to do his own healing, his own work of becoming more aware, clearer, more honest, and so on, none of us has to do it alone. The menu selections in this section include the lost art of finger painting, mirrors that turn into doorways, and how to overcome the fear of flying.

Friendship built a fire for us to huddle around, and in its glow, we warmed ourselves, found comfort, took our time. Studying the flames together, like shamans in some secret ritual, we began to discern signs of a new understanding of love, and especially romantic love, in contrast with which our former activities in that area suddenly looked like the antics of a bunch of drunk monkeys in a cage. "Courtship" takes a look at going too fast, buying lottery tickets, and carrying big sheets of plywood in a strong head wind.

It took a lot of coffee, but eventually we could envision a possibility in which we might engage in a different, less dramatic sort of courtship, without the headlong dashes and sweeping pathos and inevitable wailing in the night, and rather a bit more quietly, as a natural extension of our continuing to court our own, greater life. In fact, our friendship had, without our intending it, become a *model* of love and sanity many of us had never had before, and we began to realize that courtship would have to be the same kind of easy, heart-to-heart, "nothing special" relationship we were already practicing and enjoying with each other over steamed rice and stir-fried vegetables. For what felt like too long a time, the idea of being in love again was enough to make us want to throw up our steamed rice and stir-fried vegetables, but the new standard had taken up residence in our cells and souls and was slowly healing the hurts that had filled us with mistrust and misgivings about the future. Some of us still dreamed of reunion with former loves who danced in other galaxies; some of us found ourselves wondering about partners we had yet to meet. But all of us had been transformed by new understandings of balance and mutuality we could never again deny. The final section of the *Chronicles*, "Partnership," explores what this simple, loving connection with another might be like. It's about sex, high school touchdowns and fumbles, marriage and divorce, men who go shopping, and trees falling in forests.

My name is Philip, and I'll be your server today. If you enjoy your visit to the Grill, please tip generously, and be sure to tell all your friends.

Introduction

Our world is no restaurant and no picnic. More than ever, it seems to have got away from itself. You can see it in the sheer volume and pace of the information that blitzes us every day in the various media—television, radio, newspapers and magazines, junk mail, billboards. This endless barrage of *conclusions* about this or that has exhausted our attention and anesthetized our natural curiosity because conclusions and curiosity contradict each other. Conclusions are the business of knowing; curiosity, of not knowing. Conclusions bring us to endings; curiosity, to beginnings. Since every conclusion raises far more questions than it answers, conclusions tend to spin out faster and faster, often contradicting themselves as they go; curiosity, which likes to linger in the question, takes its time, explores, tries on different shapes, colors, and sizes. Conclusions are reached and tested through hypothesis, a systematic plan, the scientific method. Curiosity, on the other hand, precedes all plans and purposes and methods.

So conditioned are we to being-as-knowing that we've actually come to equate being *aware* with *having information*—with reading the papers and tuning in the news on the radio or television, all of which present a removed, chronically negative, and even theatrical if not sensationalist report of what's "going on in the world." But reported information alone can't make us aware. Really being aware of what's going on in the world requires that we be grounded in a much more immediate experience of what's going on in *our* world, right here, right now. Most immediately, this includes what's going on in our bodies, our emotions and thoughts, our beliefs and fantasy projections, and our sense of who we are, what we deserve, and what our life is about. We don't learn these things all at once the way we get information, by turning on the television at six o'clock or buying a newspaper. They're revealed only gradually through an inner listening, through the practice of paying attention, watching, being still so that who we are can reveal itself to us in its own time. Real awareness grows not out of our acquiring information, but out of our natural curiosity about being alive. Ultimately, our awareness itself, directed to the here and now, is our most reliable source.

Many writers, I'm told, read insatiably when they were kids. I didn't. I took things apart. Any machine or device I could get my hands on was fair game. One minute it was together, the next, in pieces. Telephones, ball-point pens (they made great rocket launchers), and my favorite, watches. I could fieldstrip a 17-jewel Bulova in twenty minutes—I'm talking *every* gear out. I never did manage to get anything back together (which has given me a chilling way to think about what we may end up doing with the atom). To this day, my brother looks at me crookedly when he reminisces at a family gathering about how I "fixed" his typewriter, and my father still won't let me near his Seiko.

Granted, my childhood curiosity had a destructive edge, and there is certainly a time to stop taking things apart, to stop analyzing, but I *had* to see what was inside, what was hidden. And I like this about myself, that I dismantled watches and other contraptions to see what made them tick even though I couldn't put Humpty together again. Putting together would have taken knowledge, technical skill, information. What I was doing was much more basic, even primal. To see the inside of things, to get past the appearance to the underlying reality. *That* was what I wanted. And that's why when I came of age and no longer took apart physical objects, I studied philosophy, where I could take apart metaphysical ones, still with the same purpose: to find the fundamental, discern the secret, uncover the "essential" that Saint-Exupéry tells us is "invisible to the eye." Since then, my beliefs have diverged from those that must have prompted Exupéry to write that lovely line. I've been learning how to let things be together, and how precious the visible, the ordinary, can be. But first I needed to go through a time of taking apart, of tearing down what old hurts and years of habit had put in the way of simply being.

Which brings us to the Sunset Grill. Now *there's* a restaurant. Sits right at the corner of Fairbanks and New York Avenue in woodsy Winter Park, Florida. On clear summer days, its atrium windows and lush ficus trees give the place the bright airiness of a tropical retreat. When it's stormy out, you can sip coffee to a panoramic view of slate gray thunderheads rolling in low, and Winter Parkers running for cover from the lightning, which actually kills about a dozen people a year in the Sunshine State. There's a slight deco feeling to the restaurant—Tetsuro Sawada prints and neon logo signs, paddle fans and hanging Tiffany lampshades adding a confident touch of mood. The servers, who wear khaki shorts or trousers, white shirts, and burgundy aprons, are casual and friendly, and the black bean soup with scallions and melted jack cheese is the next best thing you'll find to a fireplace when it's pouring outside and you're holed up at a corner table with a good book or a good friend.

Maybe it was an accident, but somehow the place became our "church." For over two years, Kären, Rick, Dennis, Gretchen, and I met religiously at the Grill to share what was going on in our lives the way we often shared a piece of Outrageous Apple Pie, taking bites in turn, wondering if the calories were worth the ride, sitting there, eating until it was all gone and we'd done it. I think we saw our lives like that, or at least, something like that. By the time we hit the end of our thirties, life was no piece of apple pie, though it was often outrageous. The Sunset Grill became a refuge where we could meet and sort things out, where we could take apart the pens and watches of our relationships with each other, with our loves and former loves, with ourselves, with being alive. We kept no secrets; we were there to be nourished and we knew it. Even when we had no idea of how to put the pieces back together, we opened ourselves and told the truth; more often, we simply sat there believing in each other as we struggled to find it.

And that's how this book, which is about love and coming home to the truth—two halves of the same enchilada—came about. In these chronicles, you'll eavesdrop on some of the countless conversations we had over breakfast and brunch and dinner and desserts when we didn't give a damn about our diets. Read at will. Stay for the whole meal, a course at a time, or order a la carte. Maybe you, too, will find something here to satisfy and nourish you.

The SUNSET GRILL CHRONICLES

HARDSHIP

The heart is a very, very resilient little muscle.

—Woody Allen
Hannah and Her Sisters

Lost and Found

When everything goes wrong, what a joy to test
your soul and see if it has endurance and courage!
—Nikos Kazantzakis
Zorba the Greek

 *Kären looks up nervously from across the table. The advancing wisps of gray hair at her otherwise jet black temples are marking runaway time and she knows it. She's just lost her job as a copywriter in a small marketing firm, and since loss of any kind always seems to resurrect the pain of the deepest loss she carries, we're soon talking about* him *again. Her eyes wince as the feelings come. She lowers her head into her hands, and the gray streaks tumble forward across the back of her long fingers. Noticing this, the approaching waiter hesitates, then discreetly turns away to tend to other chores for a few minutes. Loss. Again. Loss resurrected by loss—the passing days, another job, the man she loved, all lost to time and little episodes she wishes could be lived over differently. And I wonder: How much can a person lose without becoming, in a way, ruined? Is there a point past which injury simply cannot be undone? Going on,*

salvaging a measure of happiness or at least the basic confi-
dence that being alive is, despite everything, good and
worthwhile—it isn't as though we have a right to these things,
after all. There may be limits. And aren't we shaped far more
by what we lose than what we gain? The way events unfold,
a loss may pull us through an unexpected doorway, place our
feet on a previously unseen path, write us into a new story of
far greater depth, purpose, and accomplishment than we
could have imagined. In fact, seven difficult weeks from now,
a local magazine publisher will start interviewing for a staff
writer. Although Kären doesn't know it yet, she'll get that
job, and less than two years later, she'll have made senior
editor and achieved national recognition. This new work will
mark the beginning of a new life for her. And, of course, if she
hadn't lost the copywriting job . . .

Looking back, I found it startling how much, collectively,
our small band of friends had lived through: alcohol and
drug addiction, sexual abuse, multiple marriages and di-
vorces, long-term poverty, various "stress-related" disorders,
and a smorgasbord of dysfunctional family histories, to name
some of the biggies. We'd spent years in denial, years in counseling, and more time than we could remember being enraged, confused, and feeling like we didn't belong. In short,
we'd been playing the game of life and coming up losers.

Now, all of this losing brings to mind something that happened to me in the fourth grade, when I was ten years old.
There was a class party and everyone brought a wrapped
present to toss into a grab bag. At the end of the day, for the
big finale—god, it was thrilling—we each got to grab. When
it was my turn, I stepped up to the pillowcase, took a deep

breath, and reached in, stirring through the gifts, trying to find the one that *felt* just right, a terrific toy or something. I pulled out a small package wrapped in blue paper, then ran over to the corner of the room to open it. I remember the sick rush of disappointment when, tearing away the wrapping, I found a set of *jacks*. A dumb rubber ball and those little pewter stars that no *boy* would be caught dead playing with.

All around me, of course, were the winners—kids squealing over a model airplane or an official, glow-in-the-dark, Duncan yo-yo or a joy buzzer. Then, I noticed one of my classmates, a girl, standing off by herself, looking much the way I felt, and I walked over to her. In her hands, fresh out of the grab bag, was an ordinary pack of notebook paper— the lined, three-holed kind. So, not wanting the jacks anyway, I asked her if she felt like trading, and it was as though with those words I had raised the dead. Her eyes twinkling, she exchanged presents with me, leaving her happy and me with a pack of notebook paper.

Finally, I went up to a guy who had something really fantastic, which he tried to show me while jumping up and down; I think it was a gyroscope, or maybe a Slinky. He asked, "What did *you* get?" and I held up the paper. "Oh," he said. Then, gifted negotiator that I was even at that age, it hit me that I could go for another trade, but the words came out something like: "I don't really want this. Do you?" to which he replied with a shrug, "Sure," whereupon he snatched the paper and walked off, leaving me empty-handed and emptier-hearted. It all happened so fast, I simply didn't have the presence of mind to say, "No, no—I don't mean I want to *give* this to you, you jerk. I want to *trade*." Instead, I just stood there. Unlike Zorba, I couldn't dance in the face of head-on loss. Instead, I cried as privately as I could until the bell rang, ending the whole rotten, miserable, nosebleed of a day.

As trivial as it seems, that loss touched me to the core, which is why I remember it in detail over thirty years later. To have such hope, to care so much and work so hard, and then, because of some absurd misunderstanding, to lose it all, to watch the treasure fall from your hands—this was a theme I would come to know well through my life, as would the other members of the Sunset Grill society.

Our attempts at love, despite the particular differences, all ran more or less like this. We started out full of faith and promise and somehow ended up with jacks that turned into paper that turned into nothing. For example, one of our group, Kären, was in love with a man she could not stop rescuing from this or that crisis. Along their erotic and erratic course, he gave her many opportunities on that score, resenting her bitterly each time her "strength" did for him what he really needed to do for himself. After each rescue, or sometimes for no other reason than that his own demons just happened to be restless, he would pull away, suddenly needing "space" or drugs or alcohol or another woman when only hours or even *minutes* before he had wanted to make love and be close. Yes. No. I love you. Go away. She put up with this as long as she could, all the time struggling to understand how her unconditional devotion to this man always seemed to lead to distance and disappointment. It was as though she was expecting some sort of trade that never quite worked out.

One day he was home sick with a flu and, during her lunch hour no less, she took it upon herself to go tripping around town gathering cold remedies, including a couple of prescription drugs she had at home. When she bounded through the door of his apartment and dumped this pharmaceutical grab bag on the bed where he lay, he just looked at her and blinked. Finally, he said, or rather, screamed, "Get out! You're crazy! Get out!" which she did, with not even a pack of notebook paper for her troubles. It cut her clean through. The ungrateful bastard. How could he reject her when all she was doing was *caring* for him?

Eventually, this roller-coaster ride to nowhere led her into counseling, some soul searching, and a slow relinquishing of old habits. She came to see that trying to rescue somebody else *is* crazy—as crazy as constantly setting up the need to be rescued, which was *his* specialty. They were about as compatible as Bonnie and Clyde, and the result was a firestorm of emotional violence. She started paying more attention to his actions than his words and finally realized that her needs were being all but totally ignored. And for the first time, that wasn't good enough. She confronted him with an ultimatum: either sanity, which would have to include some form of counseling and a general cleaning up of their respective acts, or good-bye Charlie, at which point Charlie said good-bye.

We spent many evenings talking about this loss, one of the most painful she had known. Years later, it was obvious that she still loved him deeply, but would rather be without him than with him on the old, self-destructive terms. During those conversations, Kären taught me about accumulated losses, expressing with persuasive conviction her belief that we humans are simply not constituted to sustain one heartbreak after another, to just walk away from loss and "get on with it." Understandably, our tendency is to minimize or even deny pain, but sooner or later, our grieving catches up to us. We realized that we'd been running from grief most of our lives, seeking refuge in relationships that set us up for further losses. We needed to stop doing that, even if it meant being alone, for a while or forever. We needed to do our grieving so we could finally be done with it, and become aware of our own damaging patterns of craziness so we could start making better choices.

Drawing on the support we found at the Grill, Kären wisely chose to take some time to simply feel the hurt, the crushing disappointment over how compulsive she and this man had both been, and how this compulsiveness had, despite their genuine feeling for each other, doomed any chance they might have had to grow together in love. She had to admit that this wasn't the first time this sort of thing had happened to her. In fact, she'd been accumulating losses for as long as she could remember. And yet, as she slowly became quieter and, so, clearer, she realized that in all the losing, she was finding something essential.

Now, far more self-possessed, she looks back at the prescription-drugs incident, among others, and laughs, shaking her head incredulously. "I was on a rescue rampage," she says. "No wonder he was freaking out, screaming at me that I was crazy. I was. We both were."

Kären lost a relationship that was ripping the hell out of everybody's gears and found a big piece of her sanity, and this is pretty much how it's gone for everyone in our group. Our losses led us to the Grill and to friends with enough guts and love to hold up the mirror. The more we looked into that mirror, the more our hiding places and clever answers and strategies fell away. Much was lost in the process. Much needed to be lost before there could be room for the finding that followed.

This finding-in-losing is certainly not about wearing rose-colored spectacles, not about making lemonade when life gives you lemons, nor even about seeing the glass as half full instead of half empty. It's about getting quiet, paying attention, and withholding judgment long enough to experience how losing something can actually set into motion a process of change that eventually resolves the loss the way musical chords resolve each other. This is illustrated well by one of my favorite stories, about a poor farmer and his son who inherit a stallion when it comes down from the mountains one day and jumps their fence. The son is overjoyed; the father says, "Who knows what's good or bad?" The next day, the horse runs off again, and the son is devastated. The father remains calm, saying only, "Who knows what's good or bad?" The next morning, the stallion returns with a herd of wild horses behind it, which by law now belong to the farmer. The son is ecstatic, but the father says simply, "Who knows what's good or bad?" On the fourth day, the son climbs on one of the horses and is thrown for a broken leg. As the leg is being set in a cast, his father gently reminds him, "Who knows what's good or bad?" And on the fifth day, the army recruiters come through the town and take all the young men except one because of his broken leg. Here are the circles and unexpected payoffs, the quick-change artistry and punch lines waiting for us in the natural unfolding of events. A set of jacks may not be much, but it can bring happiness to one disappointed child, thereby showing another that nothing is without value. A blank package of notebook paper can do more to teach the importance of using words carefully than a hundred textbooks. And a lost love can open your heart to more love than you ever knew there was to lose.

As R. D. Laing wrote, "Who are we to decide that it is hopeless?" Some findings come long after the losses they heal. I say we stick around and find out.

As the gray in our hair continues to claim new territory, even our most showstopping wins and losses turn into yesterday's news. For Kären, the job at the magazine became the

new order, with hurrahs and kudos flying like confetti in the
Sunset Grill camp. This job had come like a little miracle, but
in a while, its focus and energy began to dissipate, like the
irrevocably dissolving memories of the relationship that had,
in its time, meant so much to her. Everything passes, every-
thing changes—sometimes while we're watching. Maybe
that's why every prize won has a trace of bittersweetness in it.
There are honeymoons, but honeymoons end and we have to
start dealing with the inevitable disappointments and con-
flicts. Friday can come skipping up to you like a kid at Coney
Island, but before you know it, it's Sunday night again and
you're setting the alarm for the Monday morning forced-
march to the office. Or three weeks after you get the sexy new
car, it's somehow become just another car; the thrill has sub-
sided, and the payments are going to be with you for a long
time. Or you go to the restaurant famished and suddenly,
you're sitting back in your chair disgusted at the thought of
food and vowing to start your diet tomorrow. Christmas
morning flashes into Christmas afternoon cleanup, and all
that anticipation is lying around the living room in shreds like
the wrapping paper that only a few hours earlier held so
much promise. These tiny revolutions go on all the time,
ousting one little regime in favor of another that will, in its
turn, be ousted, and so on. Inexorably, the new opportunity
changes into the same old grind—and we're left to regroup,
catch our breath, start over. Then, one day, a gift rises,
phoenix-like, out of the ashes of hardship. It's this discontin-
uous continuity that we can't predict. We can know what
happens, but we can't be sure of what it signifies, how it fits
into the larger concatenation of events, what will come to
pass as a result. Because we live instantly, because there's
only now, life happens before we know it, and this is the crux
of it all—this "before we know it." The path unfolds right

*under our feet; the rest is darkness and uncertainty and ed-
ucated guesswork. And we have to keep moving forward all
the same, or at least, what feels like forward. Which is why
after six years, Rick and I sold our advertising agency—fired
ourselves, in a way. It was time. Like Kären, we had to move
on, though we didn't know to what. And often, the only way
to move forward is to jump off a cliff and see what happens.
We're all cliff jumpers, even when we think we've got everything covered, everything under control. And all we can count
on is a kind of faith in flight . . .*

Self-Help, Faith, and Knowing

God doesn't want you to be certain. That's why he gave you a brain.

—Dennis Hays

 *When Rick and I sold the agency, I felt pretty sure that I'd be able to make the transition without a hitch. I had connections back into the world of teaching, my first book was doing all right and the second was nearly finished, and Kären and I felt confident about a workshop we had put together on personal/social evolution and journal keeping. There was a little money from the sale of the agency, enough to support a full-time writing/part-time teaching schedule for a couple of years. What I didn't anticipate was that, in losing the agency, I'd lose one of my biggest complaints. This would, in turn, hold up a mirror of my lifelong devotion to sadness, separateness, and struggle. And at that point, there would be a much higher cliff to jump from. When it was all done, when the agency had changed hands and we were no longer trapped in what had been for us the Dorian Gray world of advertising and marketing, the*

*hours and days and weeks that I thought would come wear-
ing garlands turned on me like the lifting rifles of a firing
squad. I scrambled to find something wrong, something that
would take me back to the safe world of discontent, and I
couldn't. Freedom, its fangs dripping, was at hand, and I
soon felt as though I were dying. Within weeks, a volley of
symptoms began ricocheting through my body and psyche:
apprehension; sharp, burning pains in the abdomen; headaches and dizziness; exhaustion; chronic difficulty in getting
a deep breath; listlessness and depression.*

*During the same time, Rick jumped across a ditch on a golf
course, landed in a mud hole, and tore his Achilles tendon
like an old rag. Not something Achilles would have done, but
there Rick was, laid up for six weeks in a full leg cast and
married to helplessness and inactivity. Dennis, Gretchen, and
Kären also seemed to be succumbing to stressful events
through autoimmune traffic jams and "accidents." Dennis
was suffering from frequent headaches and galloping insom-
nia. Gretchen developed various false-alarm symptoms.
Kären seemed unable to shake loose of a low-grade flu, a sore
throat, and pouncing financial whammies. We all had our
way of dealing with too much grief, or too little. And eventually, we'd all get to experience the truth of the saying, "Pain
is the sickness, sickness the cure . . ."*

W hat made the Sunset Grill revolutionary was that we
met solely to help ourselves. This may not seem like much,
but you have to remember a couple of things: First, we had,
without exception, spent our whole lives sabotaging ourselves, especially in matters of love. Second, we had absolutely no reason to believe that whatever was wrong with
us—and something *was* wrong—could be handled by long,

soulful talks over coffee and Crispy Coated Spiral Fries. Some of us had seen doctors who told us that what we needed to be eating was Prozac. According to them, our long-standing depression and anxiety were the products of chemical imbalances in the brain (not anybody's brain in particular, just *the* brain), but we didn't have to worry, they said. Clinical depression could now be medically managed with little pills that get up into your gray matter and fine-tune your emotional centers like a ham radio operator hounding for skip waves. Of course, when we heard that, calm and undramatic people that we are, we immediately conjured up images of unspeakable side effects, long-term use and dependency, and uh-excuse-us-but-we-just-discovered-that-this-particular-compound-plays-cat's-cradle-with-your-DNA-gee-sorry-about-that. It was a grim picture, but for all we knew, the doctors were right, and if they were, clinging to some notion of self-help would be about as productive as trying to push your way out of a phone booth.

So, to build a new life around these meetings, to take them *that* seriously, the first thing we had to do was put a stone in our slingshot and walk out to confront the Goliath of modern Western medical authority. That would have been enough of a challenge, especially when for many of us, the dust clouds of the last exploded relationship were still hanging in the air, and it took everything we had just to remember how to put our shoes on right. But there was more. To make the odds just a tad worse than they were for the biblical David, the gods gave us a second giant to contend with: the seductive claim of the so-called new age—"You create your reality." And there we were, wondering if we'd felt depressed, lost, apprehensive, and angry for years because: (a) our brains were broken, or (b) we were sloppy creators. If it turned out to be *a,* like it or not we'd have to take the drugs; if *b,* we didn't know what we'd have to do, but whatever it was, we'd have to do it differently than we ever had, and until we did, taking pills wasn't going to get to the root of it. The tremendous tension between these two Titans raised all sorts of doubts and questions about our faith and how far we were willing to go in acting on our faith, knowing that it might cost us our skin if we were wrong.

The coffee was good. The Spiral Fries seemed fine. Prozac, we weren't so sure about. We'd all heard about people who had taken antidepressants and found relief, but there were side effects: hair falling out, nausea, dizziness, weight gain, and other pleasantries, including depression itself. More than that, those we knew who had used the drugs couldn't shake the suspicion that they were treating symptoms, and sooner or later they found that they needed to decide whether or not to keep using the stuff. The doctors said that clinical depression was as much a disease as diabetes (nothing to be *ashamed* of) and likened antidepressants to insulin, in the sense that a person might have to take them for the rest of his life. Which gave us images of hair falling out for the rest of our life. The prospect of a lasting relationship with the pharmacist wasn't the lasting relationship we'd been hoping for, and we found it especially hard to accept that this might be our fate when we had Louise Hay, Bernie Siegel, Shakti Gawain, and others looking very healthy on their book jackets and telling us that our attitudes and beliefs form our reality. According to some of these writers, if we believed that we needed drugs, our experience would bear that out. If, on the other hand, we believed that we could live a depression-free life without drugs, presumably that, too, would come to pass. Many of them spelled out techniques for changing experience through the inner work of changing beliefs. We all knew people who had tried these techniques with success.

Here, in our hot little hands, was the consummate summons to self-help and the promise of an answer to our dilemma, sans side effects.

Now, this is where the wicket gets sticky, because if it's *true* that your beliefs create your experience, then *not* believing this will keep you from experiencing it. But worse, if it *isn't* true and you believe it *is,* you could end up sitting in your room meditating, visualizing, and using affirmations when what you need to save your life is radiation treatment, insulin, or Prozac. In "Do We Make Ourselves Sick?" an interview that appeared in the September/October 1988 issue of *New Age Journal,* Ken and Treya Wilber point out the danger in the view that holds, unconditionally, that we consciously or unconsciously create everything that happens to us and so should be able to heal ourselves at will:

> New age types gather around you and say things like, "Well, what are you trying to teach yourself with this disease?" You might have, say, eye cancer, and they'll say, "What are you trying to avoid seeing?" Or you might have a broken leg, and they'll say, "Why are you avoiding standing up for yourself?" Or you might have a headache, and they'll say, "Guess whose sixth chakra isn't opened?" Or you might have some heart problems, and they'll say, "Why are you avoiding God's love?" And all of this is completely magical, narcissistic, infantile, new age nonsense. . . . And, if having cancer is not devastating enough, they have the added burden . . . of thinking they have somehow brought this thing on themselves. . . . And then, worst of all, the new agers think they should try to cure the cancer with just visualization and meditation and psychotherapy. . . . And the people who use just those approaches, only those approaches, unfortunately, they die. They were killed by the new age,

by this insane idea that I create my own reality, that only spiritual causes are operative in the world, that I should be able to order the world around in thought, that physical-level cures are a source of shame and weakness.

When we read that, a few of us felt like digging out the old prescriptions we'd never had filled and screeching up to the nearest drugstore. What did we think we were doing, anyway, "talking things out" instead of following the doctor's orders or getting other professional help? We weren't trained psychologists, after all. And what if our brain chemistry *were* off? We could self-help until the cows came home; it wouldn't make a bit of difference. Whatever nature had jury-rigged in our skulls would keep squeezing out sour milk or whatever it was, and there we'd be with our affirmations and our visualizations and our untreated depression.

But we'd run our patterns long enough to reach the bottom—that place where you finally stop pointing fingers and start looking in the mirror, and we had seen that a lot of the pain we'd been through in relationships *had* come from destructively self-fulfilling beliefs and expectations. Every one of us had at least a fourth-degree black belt in emotional sabotage, and the idea that you can't reduce human life to purely mechanical causes and effects any more than you can reduce it to merely "spiritual" ones spoke to us. There had to be a balance, or so we hoped, and we trusted the voice of intuition that said that coming out of hiding and opening our hearts would carry us closer to it. Maybe this vestige of trust in ourselves and each other, fulfilled through our actions, was enough. Maybe our simply making the decision to do *something* to help ourselves, along with the insights and new understandings we found, brought about the same kinds of subtle adjustments in our brain chemistry that certain drugs are supposed to induce. Maybe the doctors were wrong. Maybe, maybe, maybe. We didn't know then and we still don't. All we know is that, as the months passed, our lives came into focus. We started letting go of old pain and began laughing more, at ourselves, each other, the foibles, the dramas we had thrown ourselves into so desperately. We began breathing and feeling more deeply, taking up a long-lost residency in our bodies. And we started to feel better, healthier, without Prozac and without knowing.

Many of our doubts were still unresolved on the bumpy road of self-help and self-transformation: How *do* you know whether or not to believe that belief creates experience? Or to undergo a certain medical treatment rather than some alternative? Or to return a phone call or letter or birthday card from a partner who keeps leaving you? The answers to these questions and other gut-wrenchers always turned out to be the same: You don't know, and you don't try to figure it out. You *listen*. That's all. And if you sit still for a while, something in your heart speaks to you and you respond. The rest is faith, and faith isn't tied to this or that outcome, because who can say what an outcome is anyway, or what's possible in the next moment? Even dying, as Socrates said, may be the greatest good that can happen to us. Faith eliminates all pretense of knowing and all second-guessing. It's unconditional— a way of saying yes to life even when the worst happens. What more can we do than "act for the best, hope for the best, and take what comes," as Fitz-James Stephen wrote? We don't know; we can't dictate, control, or sometimes even influence outcomes that mean everything to us, but we have to live through them all the same. Faith gives us a way to do that by allowing us to surrender to who we are as part of the great, continuing motion of life, and the wonderful thing is, that becomes sufficient.

There are, of course, days when the uncertainties are howl-ing, and all our faith seems like a dream we waited too long to remember. Living feels urgent again; we want to run out, phone our former wives and husbands and lovers, tell them how much we adore them, how much we hate them, remarry them, kiss them, kill them, do everything we didn't do and undo everything we did. Instead, we call each other and head for the Grill, where we remind ourselves that there's much more to our story than any one chapter, and to keep sitting still in the middle of the noise, keep listening, that's all. Then, we order cheese omelettes and home fries and orange juice and pretty soon, our faith is back. We've also found that it helps to take a slow, deep breath and in your best Jackie Mason voice, say to yourself several times: "How do you like that, I'm feeling crazy again." This mantra doesn't always spark intuition; often, it's followed by a great, mystical si-lence in which, if you listen closely, you can hear God scratch-ing His head to the theme music of "Final Jeopardy." Which is appropriate enough, since the questions are much more important than the answers anyway. Aren't they?

"Be careful what you ask for as you will surely get it," the saying warns, or as George Bernard Shaw noted, there are two tragedies in life: not getting what you want and getting what you want. True enough. As when, right after I left the agency, I came down with a bad case of the emotional D.T.s and found myself unhinged in a psychic free-fall with no one to answer to but my spirit. The nervous strain caused by this newly imposed freedom irritated the hell out of the cowboy in me who thinks that my purpose in life is to get thrown from snorting broncos, spit lead all over Dodge, kill many men, pleasure many women, and beat the crap out of the warring Indian nations single-handedly without once suffer-

ing a doubt, shedding a tear, shivering a shiver, or peeing in my pants. This cowboy, I have learned, is one fucked-up buckaroo.

Now, Gretchen is much better at feeling things than I am. When her spirit is in pain, the tears are usually right there. This is especially astonishing to me since, for years, she's headed up the Seminole County program that represents abused children in court. A normal week for her would be just about anybody else's house of horrors. And yes, sometimes she's a little too strident, a little too political, and I know that she's formed a special attachment to one of the kids, or that she's too angry to let her anger be anger, or that something else is trapped inside her psyche and is tying nightmares together like sheets to lower itself out the nearest window and head for high ground. But to an amazing extent, after almost ten years of hacking away in that terrible, dark forest, she can still feel what she's doing. And I know that she's endured this work by staying utterly open and vulnerable to this world and what it does to its children. Someday, I think, I'll be that free, too . . .

He/She

When I was a little girl,
there was a way that I was.
I could feel.
I could feel the stars.

—Kären Neustadt

 *Dennis is a good photographer. He can take a picture of a piece of white canvas against a blue sky and make it look like the foreground and background are having sex. His photos have captured the clandestine geometry of drainpipes in a forgotten alley, the droning fury of a stock-car race, the buzzing torpor of a lazy, front-porch afternoon in the Old South. Dennis is in love with images. But this important part of his character is a flower that's rooted in dark soil, because his early life scared the hell out of him, and he learned that he could, through the magic of picking up a camera, remove himself to the safety zone of the witness. By looking through the viewfinder, Dennis takes himself out of the picture and escapes into the illusion of not-being-there. It's an illusion because the photographer is, of course, always present as the point of view that frames the shot, that anchors it in time and space. Still, old habits die hard, and Dennis prac-*

ticed the Invisible Man routine into his forties. When I ran into him during a wintry Chicago business trip after ten years without contact between us, I was jolted. He looked about as close to postmortem as I ever want to see. His eyes had retreated into deep, foreboding shadows; he seemed precariously balanced, quietly desperate. He told me that he had no friends, no money, no automobile, no work, and certainly no sense of purpose or direction. We sat in that hotel restaurant drinking decaf for a couple of hours. Finally, it was time for me to get back, and I suggested offhandedly that he move to Florida, which he did in a few months. That meeting, he told me later, proved to be a turning point. Because the night I saw him in Chicago, he'd already decided to kill himself.

Last week, Dennis and I were driving along a roller coaster of a two-lane country road (it's a treat to find anything resembling a hill in central Florida), when he suddenly pulled halfway onto the shoulder, grabbed his camera, and got out of the car. There we were, perched in a perfect blind spot at the top of a hill, and I was afraid that we'd get smacked from behind, so I jumped out and ran back a ways from the car to wave traffic around us. Meanwhile, Dennis had jogged over to where he could take the photo he'd seen—a wide-angle shot of the road snaking away from us, with row after row of telephone poles on either side. He explained that the lens he was using would flatten out the depth of the scene, making the poles look as if they were stacked against each other like bundles of kindling. As we drove back toward the city, we watched masses of sky darken and move together over us like converging warships. The first heavy drops hit the windshield, letting us know we were in for a real downpour, and Dennis started talking about how incredible it is that we live on a planet where water falls from the sky, as though it were some sort of miracle. He went on like this, and he seemed like such *a kid, so innocent, snapping his pictures and rhapsodizing about the rain. Then, I remembered how he had looked that night in Chicago, when it was ten below outside and he'd taken a bus to meet me. And I thought, hills come up just like that and cars come up behind you just like that and storms come up just like that. You've got to watch how you go. Just like that, you can find yourself spinning out toward the edge of the world. Then, it's up to luck and grace and grit whether or not you manage to outlive the heartache and find your way back to the center. And I thought, no, he's not a kid, not innocent, not anymore. He's alive. And not a minute too soon.*

There are two things that every writer has to deal with eventually: life and pronouns. Some years ago, after a pronoun crisis too painful to go into here, I decided to stick with *he* and, for the most part, avoid the devilish *he or she* that Fowler, among others, advises against. I'd learned that, despite the prodding of feminism, there was no way to use this *he or she* as often as it seemed to come up without creating so much stylistic awkwardness that it just wasn't worth it. Good writing is music, I figured, and if the lyrics start upstaging the melody, they have to go. Keeping company with the male pronoun also made sense to me because I happen to *be* male, and using *he* serves to remind me that, even when I seem to be talking about other people, I'm really only talking about myself, about how I see them.

Actually, the issue here isn't about *male* and *female* at all but *masculine* and *feminine,* which have little to do with anatomy. These terms identify two, deep-running rivers in the human psyche that course through each of us, regardless of our gender, for spiritually speaking, we are all *both* masculine and feminine: visible and hidden, penetrating and receptive, resolute and yielding, soft as silk and tough as nails. And the question of how to realize ourselves increasingly, how to become more and more fully who we are—more "individuated," as Jung called it—is in practice, the question of how to rediscover the natural integrity and balance of our complete sensuousness and spiritual androgyny.

On all sides, masculine and feminine energies commingle in a great cosmic romp that produces life as we know it, or think we know it. These two complementary qualities show up in varying degrees to make a thing what it is. Hard and soft, in and out, give and take, potatoes and patatas—we can see the he/she dance going on in everything from the nervous little sneezes of subatomic charges to the lumbering ballet of galaxies. Even the body itself may be thought of as feminine in relation to the awareness that permeates and quickens it, which is masculine. In this way, the body and awareness belong together as do lovers. When these two "come" together, there is life, presence, responsiveness, a certain focus in the here and now; conversely, if awareness withdraws too far from the body, as it does in drunkenness, chronic emotional denial, autism, coma, and other compromised conditions, both seem to suffer in the separation. The imagery here is necessarily sexual, or perhaps it's better to say that sex *embodies* in a kind of sensory language, the prior spiritual truth that the body is the womb of awareness. This primal union of flesh and feeling is given to us; it is not a function of our will. We can't *make* ourselves be in our body any more than we can make ourselves go to sleep. But we can *let* ourselves be in our body, in our senses—facing, accepting, and expressing the truth of our inner life rather than, say, trying to live up to somebody else's idea of who we are, or otherwise tugging at the masculine reigns of misplaced effort.

Most of what's basic in life is brought about and sustained through this effortless cooperation with what is already present, through the mysterious, hidden efficiencies of the feminine: breathing, thinking, transmuting food into living tissue, being in a body at all, the turning of the planet and the seasons—no one has to *do* any of this, yet, somehow, it all gets done, and with a precision that our best planning could only hinder. In this spirit, as far as I can tell, the *Tao Teh Ching* says, "Do nothing and everything will be done," or in the words of Lien Gway Chang, the world-renowned T'ai Chi master, "I do nothing, so there is nothing I cannot do." By this "doing nothing," that is, by cultivating an alert receptivity, willingness, and watchfulness, the power of the feminine can be evoked and released into a situation, often with remarkable results. Even a little letting go goes a long way.

But we don't like this "not doing." We're busy people with busy schedules in a busy world. And many of us keep the busyness going in order to drown out what our bodies keep trying to tell us—that we're running away from our emotions, our vulnerability, and most of all, our old, unresolved pain. Filled with the inner static of opinions, beliefs, plans, prejudices, conditioning, desires, expectations, fears, and fantasies, we have little room left in us for *us,* for a direct, unobstructed experience of ourselves as we are, in the living moment. Now, all of this running around is pure willfulness, and willfulness always needs to be balanced *through the power of the feminine.* To rediscover this balance, to experience the fullness of the moment at hand and ourselves in it, we need *willingness*—the willingness to look and see, to listen and hear, to acknowledge inner and outer events as they are. This willingness to let life present itself in this way is our connection to the bestowing power of the feminine, which reveals us to ourselves in the same way that physical objects are revealed by the space in which they are extended. It is the feminine that gives us room to live, to be. But we need to remember that this term isn't tied to gender. The passive woman clings to the victim role just as willfully as the macho man clings to the role of the emotionless, controlling hero. Despite appearances and popular opinion, both suffer from the same spiritual constriction and imbalance: excessive willfulness, or a denial of feminine awareness and practice.

The more we talked over so-called men's and women's issues at the Grill, the more we realized that we had arrived pretty much at the same place. We were all stuck, to whatever degree, out of touch with our bodies and emotions; we were all hurt, afraid, and angry; and we had spent our adult life taking that out on our partners, all of whom were now former partners. This glaring common denominator had been hidden by the fact that as men and women, we had been sent into bodily exile via different routes.

Consider the male: For decades, sexism was defined largely as the oppression of women by men. More recently, the quiet violence perpetrated against males in our society has been coming to light—a violence that made the oppression of women, children, other males, animals, and even the earth itself, inevitable. A female is robbed of her masculine power to act, her sense of competence, her right to choose and earn and be taken seriously. A male, on the other hand, is robbed of only one thing: his body. Now, by "body," I mean the *middle*—the heart, stomach, and guts, where emotions take place spontaneously and naturally, where they rise and fall and let you know you're alive. How is this crime perpetrated? By breaking the male's *feminine* spirit, by systematically teaching him to deny his emotions any psychic room in which to occur. This training is reinforced in school where other young males, who are also having their bodies amputated, jeer things like "Don't you have any guts?" and so on if a boy shows fear or sadness. This shit nicely fertilizes his growing belief that acceptance by those who matter most in his life—his parents and peers—depends on his ability to get out of his heart, his gut, his stomach, to leave his body behind in a never-never land called "manhood." It's no wonder that Peter Pan didn't want to grow up, and that the problem of the *puer aeternis*—the eternal youth—is so widespread among so-called adult males in our society. Boys will be boys, unless, of course, they're not allowed to be, in which case, men will be boys. Count on it.

While males are forced to short-circuit their emotions in order to be "men," their intellect and genitals are left more or less intact to serve as convincing substitutes for the genuine feeling-areas of the body later in life. And these two "heads" often become weapons through which all kinds of buried anger and control-missiles get fired off, simply because the man can't feel and he's mad as hell about it. This prepares him well to be a soldier and fight wars, compete aggressively in business, and in general, battle his way through being.

The political oppression of the female is really a social and political manifestation of the violence that has been done to the male psyche. Both men and women have encouraged this violence unwittingly by accepting beliefs that reinforce the disincarnation of the male spirit. Take the idea, for example, that only women fake orgasms, which, as Michael Ventura points out, is absurd. An orgasm is not the same as merely "coming," which, presumably, a man can't fake very convincingly, at least not if the woman is paying attention. To have an orgasm is not merely to come, but to experience deep love and emotional union with another, an event that may coincide with the act of coming but certainly doesn't have to, and can commence long before and last long after the physical release. In fact, men fake orgasms all the time, and the tragedy is that they don't even know they're faking because, not being aware of their bodies, they have no standard for comparison. That's why if you ask a man what he feels, he'll tell you what he _thinks_ every time. Worse, he thinks that _is_ feeling.

In its simplest form, the shutting down of the male psyche begins with some form of "Big boys don't cry," but this quickly extends to the expression of other emotions, including love. I remember how hurt I felt when, after turning thirteen, I tried to kiss my father as I always had, only to be stiff-armed by a handshake. (Now, if I move fast, I can plant one right on his lips, at which point he usually stifles a grin, shoves me away, and starts yelling at my mother.) This stoic temperament is a hangover of rugged individualism and the pioneer spirit, John Wayne biting on a bullet while they pull out the arrow, go ahead, Doc, do it clean. And if this were all there was to it, most men probably would be _in_ their bodies instead of giving them up to heart attacks, ulcers, cancer, strokes, compulsive work, alcoholism, and suicide. No such luck. The difficulty for the emerging male identity is compounded by the fact that being a man does involve a certain grounding in traditionally masculine values: the ability to face adversity, to assert, to take a stand—which means to stand up for some things and, if necessary, against others. The male psyche constellates around this archetypal urge toward assertiveness, even heroism, and this urge can't be denied without harm to a man's spirit. Without some sense of the heroic, some trace of the warrior, his life becomes vapid and dull, a mere existence.

There are primal forces within us greater than our ideas about who we are. As Greek tragedy teaches, the gods will not be denied, and refusing to honor these forces has exacted a walloping price from us all. It is certainly a modern tragedy that we have failed to appreciate how deeply a true warrior values the feminine within himself so that he can feel and draw upon the power of his emotions, choose his battles, yield when yielding is wiser, and empathize with, even grieve for, those who fall by his hand. Without this kind of generosity of spirit, which can show itself in the most mundane act of kindness or honesty, there is no heroism and no hope for the male spirit. Instead of making a little room for this, we've allowed ourselves and our children to be victimized by an intergenerational sales pitch that glorifies the image of the warrior without the warmth. So, we take pride in having splattered the flesh and blood of hundreds of thousands of Iraqis, and our national response is essentially indistinguishable from a Super Bowl victory celebration. This is what it has come to. Through this theft of our femininity and our feelings, the true warrior in us has been bound and gagged. In his place has arisen a caricature-self for whom winning is everything, which is the way not of warriors but of dogs fighting over meat.

Although many of us had mothers who showed us what feeling looked like, we could only follow them so far. As John Lee, director of the Austin Men's Center, says, men have to learn how to feel from other men. This is built into the nature of role-modeling. In fact, our mothers, by openly expressing their feelings, only confirmed the conditioning coming from dear old Dad, that showing emotion is womanly. So, we gave up our bodies and our feelings to be like fathers who were not around, or not emotionally around, who never cried or danced with joy, who never expressed their pain or encouraged us to express ours, while our mothers and sisters provided the final proof that feeling is female.

Which brings us to women. Women are taught to express

emotions by *their* role models, and not surprisingly, are often accused of being "hysterical" by men who, it must be kept in mind, are terrified of feelings. In fact, the root of this word, *hystera*, comes from the Greek for "womb" because it was believed that a certain disorder of this organ produced hysteria. To this day, there are a lot of men who can't get past the idea that a woman in the Oval Office would have periods, as though that's all she'd be doing there. Now, given that little girls are at least not discouraged from having and expressing feelings as part of their identity, one might be tempted to think that women don't have any problems in this area, which isn't true—somehow both sexes get disconnected from their bodies and their emotions.

So, if women aren't psychically disenfranchised from their bodies practically from the starting line, as men are, how do they end up on the outs? The sad fact is, women are so deeply hurt by the violence of victim/passivity conditioning, by unfeeling fathers and wounded mothers, and later, by unfeeling husbands, that their natural confidence and self-esteem plummet. The void created by this plummeting is filled with shame, feelings of inadequacy, fear, self-doubt, and a deep sense of obligation to live life once removed. These are the *real* feelings churning deep down inside the female body, feelings so painful that by the time the little girl becomes a young woman, she will have learned long ago to turn them off. And in their place, she'll substitute a repertoire of dramatic reactions, soap-opera histrionics (unrelated to *hystera*), a kind of "emoting" or acting out that often takes the form of needy attachment to a man, who, remember, can't feel emotion, but through whom she hopes to find the emotional fulfillment that her conditioning has made impossible. Her fear in the face of an overpowering "man's world" and the anger she was always taught "nice girls" don't express wind up in the deep freeze. And here is where East and West meet, for unlike the young male, she is not forced to model numbness and a contrived indifference, and probably will manage to retain some access to her body's emotional signals, but just like the male, she must learn to jam these signals to comply with a world that repeatedly hands her emotional pain and continually denies her direct expression of what she feels. Instead, she is taught to live up to an image of virtue, charm, and "femininity." Since these imposters are inconsistent with her natural, direct emotional expression of herself, she must acquire the skills of *indirect* expression, and this becomes as much a matter of her sense of her identity as nonexpression is for the male. Consequently, she indirectly expresses her anger in passive-aggressive behavior, cold shoulders, silent treatments, a catalog of victim faces and postures, "bitchiness," sexual withholding, and sometimes feigned virtue, all as a way of either getting what she wants or hurting back. Despite the early permission she had to feel and show emotion, as the indoctrination takes hold and is reinforced at school and, later, in the workplace, she comes to depend on this indirectness more and more. She finds her true feelings unacceptable or simply too much to feel, let alone express, and she begins, at some point, to act out in various moods the socially approved psychodramas that are condescendingly considered by men to be "a woman's prerogative." The worst of this is that, because of the efficiency of her denial and especially because it appears as though she *is* emotionally connected, she is practically doomed to mistake these sanctioned reactions for the genuine emotions they mask in exactly the same way men mistake thought for feeling.

Women frequently sense that men are terrified of a woman's emotional power, which they have to be since they're afraid of their own, and that if they show this power, their men will leave, which they may. This comes out of the insidious and rampant propaganda that says a woman is attractive and lovable as long as she's a little girl—that is, as long as she's emotionally powerless. Her willingness to play this role, of course, only encourages the man to stay stuck in his excessive masculinity, and as these roles are enacted, deep resentments brew on all sides. The game finally falls apart because, although the man finds the little-girl routine charming and flattering to his ego in the beginning, he eventually resents being held responsible for the woman's happiness and for her often mercurial and unpredictable moods. Men eventually reject these little girls, just as women eventually withdraw from the men they marry when these men, far more terrified than it ever appeared, turn out to be what seem like heartless little boys whose attention span isn't a whole lot longer than the time it takes to come. Caught in this role, disconnected from their real emotions, women are no more in their bodies than men are, or not much more. They, too, are afraid to face the enormous depth of their long-buried rage and grief, and so they impersonate feeling, while men, afraid of everything including their own emotional power and the emotional power of women, impersonate feeling by either thinking or ejaculating. Because both sexes have been psychically overcontrolled, both lose themselves and, inevitably, each other in the bargain. And both end up heartbroken and cynical about love and partnership.

This is not to deny that men may have to approach the problem of getting back in touch with their bodies one way, women another. There are real differences in social training between men and women, and perhaps even differences in psychological and emotional makeup, whatever they may be. But as our talks at the Grill continued to lead us out of the closet of gender-brainwashing, we found it exciting to realize that men and women are essentially struggling to get to the same place, to a vibrant and unobstructed embodiment of their emotional experience in the here and now, and that they have this crucial task in common. What has been called the "battle of the sexes," then, seems to contain the seeds of an incredible, perhaps unprecedented collaboration in healing.

How can we bring this healing about? First, by understanding what it means to be numb to our bodies, unable to feel our feelings, to be sleepwalking, emotionally absent, impersonating ourselves. Many of us had been like this our entire adult life. By the time we hit our late thirties, we also hit the skids. The habits we'd always relied on to deny and pollute reality, habits that had us more than we had them, started to wear thin, and the fear, shame, and grief we'd stuffed and swallowed and run from began to percolate into awareness. Some of us experienced this as a vague but persistent uneasiness, a sense that we were on the outside of life looking in, that we didn't belong in our skin. For others, it was more intense, but either way, for the first time, we could feel how little we had really felt. Something big was trying to get our attention. And we knew that if we looked at it, it would change us forever.

When we stopped resisting our own feelings, when we slowed down and let our psyche know that it could have all the room it wanted, some surprising things happened. One night, for example, I cried for two hours as I watched *Babes in Toyland,* an old Laurel and Hardy movie I hadn't seen since I was a boy, and I can't tell you why except that it was so much a part of me. The film opens with Victor Herbert's melody and lyrics, which I had memorized, it seemed, lifetimes ago: "Childhood joyland—mystic, merry Toyland/ Once you pass its borders, you can ne'er return again." As I listened, my stomach and throat filled with grief for the loss of my youth, for so many years spent in exile from my body, for the wounds I had both inflicted and suffered in my attempts at closeness with women—attempts that had been throttled by so much stowed anger and fear. And as this grief rose and subsided, I sensed a profound restoration of inner order that left me exhausted, but also physically and emotionally more lucid, more present, more alive, than I had been in decades. I felt as though I'd come home.

Sexism is, in the end, only another symptom of our homesickness, and we won't move beyond it until we let awareness ease back into our body and start allowing our emotions some room to be, just as they are. Since this is precisely what both men and women have been taught not to do, and since allowing room is a feminine skill, clearly, the feminine lead is the one to follow at this historical hour, especially with the threat of a thermonuclear accident (or an on-purpose) spinning over our planet like some high-tech Sword of Damocles. This, along with acts of terrorism, political duplicity, opportunistic and exploitive foreign policy, and environmental strong-arming, shows us on a global scale the sort of chaos we may expect in our personal lives if we refuse to return to the feminine. Without the reintegration of the feminine in the human psyche, we're on thin ice, whatever our pronoun.

American Indians believed that God is a trickster and that, at the last minute, just when it looks as though the spirit has been vanquished, He will appear and pull the rug out from under those who have let themselves become complacent and heartless. Then, with a wave and a laugh, He'll turn the whole shebang around and restore the eternal truths in history. The story is profound when you consider that for all the progress we've made, for all our claims to being civilized and advanced, we've created an epidemic of confusion, depression, dissatisfaction, fear, and maladjustment—"all the modern inconveniences," as Twain put it. Maybe the Indians were right. Maybe the Trickster has been working His magic all along, and still has a few awful cards up His sleeve. But what we are willing to face, we may not have to be forced to face. There may still be time for us, men and women, to open ourselves to the restorative and balancing power of the feminine—to practice receptivity, willingness, patience, and attentiveness to our inner voices so that we can recognize the ones among them that are really our own, and infuse our actions with an awareness of the truth of our being. If we do this, maybe we can beat our pronouns into plowshares and appease the Trickster-God before it's too late.

Contrary to the popular metaphor, the camera is less like an eye than like a vagina and uterus. By letting in the quickening pulses of light and holding them within its nurturing darkness (too much light destroys—one can't survive a direct look at the face of God), the camera demonstrates the profoundly creative power of the feminine. A good photographer rides that power, following rather than leading. He lets the seed-form of the image develop according to its natural gestation, and when the moment is right, a picture is born. With pictures, as with love, you don't make *this happen, you let it happen.*

The other night, Dennis dreamed that he was emancipating several manacled women whose faces he couldn't recognize. This is how a man goes about finding the lost woman in himself, the woman he needs to become before he can be wholly who he is, the woman who, in the end, can save him from suicide: He takes pictures during the day and has liberation dreams at night. If he does this long enough, he may come to recognize that there really isn't any way to be "out" of the world, to be the disembodied, unfeeling witness. Like it or not, we're participants, which means that the so-called objective witness is just one more subject, one more role in the cosmic play. Dennis believes that a truly great picture is almost never planned, that it just "shows up." But this doesn't mean that the photographer receives it passively, the way the film does, for example. No, he, too, has to show up. He has to be out looking for the shot, available to it. He has to be open, alert, attentive, ready, responsive. And he has to catch it in that flash point before it all disappears.

FRIENDSHIP

Our circle is small,
rich in heart, mindful of the day's
*   textures,*
innocent, guilty, all.
The bread we break forms lines about
*   our eyes.*
Our promises have lips of red and
*   shimmering, sea-gold hair.*
They take each other as playmates and
*   bless us*
again and again
with sacred names we hear as chimes,
and bits of ice to love the summer with.
                    —Philip Golabuk
                    "The Gathering"

Finger Painting

Let It Be.

—Song Title,
John Lennon and Paul McCartney

 *Years ago, before he sidestepped into the mad world of advertising, Rick studied painting at the Chicago Art Institute. Full of creative passion, he'd planned to be a full-time artist, but waiting on tables at night and starving during the day deflated that idea fast. So, he left Chicago, but kept painting part-time and eventually developed an unusual technique of applying several layers of iridescent oil or acrylic, then scraping the canvas with small sculpting tools until the underlayers showed through. Most of his works are figurative, populated by vague, shrouded characters devoid of detail or personality, which gives them a universal and solitary presence. These beings often have their backs to the viewer as they interact with others of their kind in extraterrestrial landscapes, usually around a central, dramatic feature—a mountain, a pillar of fire, an altar. Ancient symbols line up like wraiths along the horizon and into the*

glittering sky of this dreamworld: crescent moons, crosses, six-pointed stars—symbols that tease mythic consciousness from the depths of the psyche the way the scraping brings forth the hidden layers of color underneath.

Kären paints, too, but her artistic vocabulary is entirely different from Rick's. Her medium is watercolor, and she paints bright, expressionistic windowpanes that seem to find their form more in the interaction of water, pigment, and paper than through any technique. They offer no profound symbolism, no twilight specters, no unsettling bass-tone of associations, nor do they impart a sense of ritual or myth. In Kären's work, color has primacy over content, or rather, color becomes the content. Now, the appealing thing about water-color is its transparency. You don't just see the color, you also see through *the color to the canvas, to the side that's hidden from view by an opaque medium such as oil. While Rick works with paint sculpturally, scraping away layers to reveal what's underneath, Kären uses a translucent medium and feathery style to place what's underneath right out there in the open. Both artists, employing dramatically different treat-ments, create an opening through which we can see some-thing previously hidden. Rick finds this opening in muscular color—color that shoves its way through all that would cover it; Kären finds it in gossamer washes and lines more gestured than drawn, and even emphasizes the innocence of this del-icately implied reality by using nursery room colors—muted pinks, blues, and lavenders reminiscent of the child's world. "It isn't easy to return to the rich, simple vision we had as children," she says. "It was given then, but now, we have to earn it, practice it, which means practicing the joyful imme-diacy and focused, trusting participation children have by nature. A lot of artists seem to feel that you have to be hurt-*

*ing to paint well, to paint deeply. That isn't true for me. I
didn't start painting well until I'd put the pain behind me.
The idea that creativity can only pour out of tragedy, out of
resistance, out of some great tear in the fabric, isn't a rule. In
my case, the more whole I feel, the better I paint. My most
important work takes place in an emotional climate of joy.
And the basis of this joy is an inner friendship with something
greater, something brilliant . . ."*

The word *friend* is tied in meaning to the words *love* and
free, also to *Friday,* that day we all love so much because for
most of us it ushers in forty-eight hours of freedom from all
the things we have to do the rest of the week. Monday, on the
other hand, is nobody's friend. It means back to the office,
back to school, back to the same old grind. Moan-day.

As I recall, school wasn't so bad in the second grade, especially on Friday, which was finger painting day. I can still
remember the bright primary colors in their cool plastic jars,
that unmistakable vinyl smell when you unscrewed the lids,
and best of all, the *glissade* your hands made when you
smeared that stuff out on white paper in a creamy coat of
unfingered possibility. Then, of course, came the slick, racing
knuckle-scribbles through red and yellow fields, the palm-
presses that showed the few lines little hands have, the
bunched fingertip jabs that created tiny petal-patterns where
the paper showed through the paint. It was a completely
absorbing activity in which mind, spirit, and body blended in
the simple freedom of playfully creating by getting out of the
way and letting be. No resistance, no agenda, no real objective or conclusion, no one giving orders—just a process of
moving in easy cooperation with what's at hand. Finger paint-

ing, like friendship, provides a medium for bringing something deeper to the surface.

Now, let's take leave of my finger painting class and come forward in time to the fourth grade, to 1958, the year, you may recall, that I reached into the grab bag and pulled out a set of jacks. It was also the year I met Alfred Krever, the first *best* friend I ever had. Alfred and I best-buddied our way through the Cub Scouts, the infamous berry-eating incident, and our sixth-grade play with Mike Lembeck and Harvey Weinig. Our friendship even survived the day we were out on the playground and Alfred made the mistake of telling me that he had to pee, whereupon I insisted on playing a game of follow-the-leader that would have burst the bladder of Sir Lancelot: curb-jumping, hopping up and down along high walls, squat-thrusting—with Alfred laughing and begging for mercy all the way, and me laughing so hard that *I* nearly peed. Our shenanigans lasted for three years, ending abruptly the day my family packed up our 1957 Chevy and left New York's lashing winters and slowly building inventory of buried relatives to move to Florida.

Come to think of it, the infamous berry-eating incident may have been Alfred's revenge for that game of follow-the-sadist. Here's what happened: Alfred and I were walking home as usual from P.S. 206 in Queens when suddenly he said, "C'mere, I want to show you something." He led us to a thicket of bushes laden with dark berries, then explained, "You can *eat* these." *"Really?"* I whispered, as he pulled a few off the branch and tossed them into his mouth. I watched wide-eyed. Alfred's confidence was flawless as he chewed, swallowed, and smiled broadly. The juice had already tinted his teeth a light, filmy blue, but he obviously wasn't dead, and when ten whole seconds had passed and he still wasn't dead, that was good enough for me. Friday was at hand—freedom, epic heroism, the camaraderie of explorers ice-picking their way up unforgiving glacial walls, besting treacherous seas, solving Sphinxian riddles. And so we ate abundantly of the fruit of the vine. And it was good.

Cub Scouts are supposed to do camping-out-along-the-trail things like eating berries off bushes, and it was an adventure of the first order—until I got home. "It's Alfred," my mother said, waving the phone receiver. "Hi," I said, to which my best friend, in waning tones, replied, "My stomach hurts. Maybe I was wrong about the berries. I think they were poison. Anyway, if you stick your finger down your throat you can make yourself throw up."

Now, I don't know who came up with this stick-your-finger-down-your-throat business, but I can tell you that it doesn't work. When the panic subsided and my blood quit turning to bleach, I tore into the bathroom and tried several times to stick my entire arm down my throat, cursing Alfred between gags, and I mean *gags*. It sounded like I'd swallowed the cat. For twenty minutes, I did all I could to induce vomiting via the Krever Maneuver, but all I got for my trouble was a wrenching pain in the groin—on top of having been poisoned. Fifteen minutes of trying to turn myself inside out failed to produce a single berry. Finally, I lay down on the bed and waited to die, which I didn't. That night I called Alfred back and was sorry to learn that his stomach was feeling much better. "Guess the berries were okay," he said. I guess they were.

It's funny now, but it wasn't funny then. When it comes to feeling alone and helpless, there probably isn't much that rivals the experience of finding out that you've been poisoned. Suddenly, there's an enemy *inside* you—in your skin, your body, your blood. You can reach down your throat or drink raw eggs or call the poison control center, but ultimately, it's you and the poison and time. Which plays some pretty haunting chords on the great pipe organ of the psyche because, at the risk of sounding like Rod Serling, you might say that ". . . mortality is itself a kind of poison, a usually slow-acting agent for which there's no known antidote. And we are, each of us, alone in that primary predicament—no one can be born for us, no one can die for us. Not even friendship can build a bridge across this chasm of our absolute aloneness in being mortal, not even . . . in the Twilight Zone."

So, we're all going to die; we can't smooth a pretty color over that one. But the more pressing question is whether or not we're going to live. Many of us aren't alive; we're too caught up, cut off, shut down, burned out, or pushed around. We may have everything *but* our life. It's as though someone took away our jars of finger paint and locked them up in a cabinet somewhere. Now, many Mondays later, we've forgotten how to let ourselves be, how to play, how to participate wholeheartedly in the moment. Instead of tearing open our pigments, pouring them out in plain view, and having at it, we're spending our days drawing dreary circles in our own gray matter with such colorless materials as self-judgment, guilt, worry, the shoulds and shouldn'ts of old habits, and on and on. Freud painted us into this dismal picture when he characterized the so-called unconscious as a dark repository of repressed urges steaming in the great pressure cooker of the psyche. In some ways, this is even more frightening than the mortality metaphor. It claims that the wellsprings of our psychic life are malignant. From the very beginning, we've been invaded, set against ourselves, poisoned. And we can't even stick our finger down our throat (not that it would work anyway). All we can do is pay a psychoanalyst a lot of money to stick *his* finger down our throat so that, after many years, we can throw up as much of the repressed "material" as possible. This is, of course, the doctrine of original sin and salvation in therapeutic clothing. To whatever extent we accept this misanthropic view, we will deem our inner life inherently untrustworthy if not downright dangerous, and will subsequently try to lose ourselves in outer distractions, outer surrogates, and outer authority until our existence becomes one long Monday, and the natural colors and exuberance of our identity fade slowly into the sunset of paranoid psychoanalytic thinking. So much for Freud-day.

The idea of a hostile unconscious isn't limited to psychoanalysis. It's also a chief weapon of political oppression, by which, for example, women, blacks, Jews, Palestinians, Kurds, and other groups throughout the world have been taught to view themselves as second-class citizens. Treating someone as though he doesn't have any rights, dignity, or real creative power isn't nearly as damaging as getting him to *believe* he doesn't. Once you've done that, he'll pick your cotton, cook your meals, build your pyramids, or fight your wars on command. The poison is in place. You can put down the whip. You won't be needing it.

In the most intimate *polis,* the home, psychic poison takes the form of shame, a particularly nasty concoction. Because shame convinces a person that he's fundamentally flawed, it works with the same cruel efficiency as Freud's unconscious or the psychic yoke of oppression politics to keep the paints locked away and the spirit bound, if not broken. Teach a child that making mistakes is bad, that wanting things (such as sex) is disgraceful, that being close is dangerous, or that there's something essentially suspect, if not sinful, about the other natural squiggles of the psyche, and you've turned him into a hard-core Freudian in the twinkle of an id. Suspicious of the rich tones and textures of his own inwardness, *afraid* of them, he'll look to external cues for any sense of how to move through life, and be forced by his fearful belief to color by number rather than finger paint.

Freedom—like finger painting, sex, and birth—is messy. Lots of liquids and squooshing and fast changes. To be free, to be friends with ourselves, to love our life and what we're creating each day, we have to be willing to make mistakes, to learn, to smear it around and see what happens, to let it be, to wipe it smooth and do it again and again and again. And if our work seems colorless, if we're put off by what we've become, if being alive isn't fun anymore, maybe it's because we've insisted on keeping our hands too clean.

Alfred didn't worry about clean. He played and laughed and jumped around even when he had to pee, because he knew that being comfortable isn't the most important thing. He ate the magic berries (ate them *first*) because he knew that playing it safe isn't the most important thing. And he phoned right away to tell me a messy truth, to paint a picture of himself as a jerk and save my life, because he understood that looking good isn't the most important thing. That U-turn, which, in half an hour, took us from the heights of heroism to the depths of dread, was an act of wholehearted friendship and love, and some of the best finger painting I've ever seen. It's also why, after thirty years without contact, Alfred Krever is still a best friend of mine.

As with finger painting, living and loving well depend on a certain amount of improvisation. And we can't improvise if we haven't made friends with whatever we have to work with. Imagine standing over an excited, enthusiastic six-year-old who's holding up his newly finished masterpiece and saying to him, "This is too red; the lines are too wide; you should have coated the paper more evenly with the paint." Yet, isn't this how the voice in our head talks to us much of the time, a voice we may still be mistaking for our own? But this voice is not our own, not a voice that can show us how to be our own best friend, not a voice that loves us and encourages us to explore freely the shadows and highlights of our own, spontaneous identity. Far from it, this is the voice of old enemies, of Monday morning agendas—the voice that rejects or slanders what we love and poisons what is best in us: our passion, our courage, our capacity for improvisation.

We may feel that our childhood was too traumatic, that we got too many bad breaks, that our colors are too dark to touch, that we carry too many years of heartache, loss, disappointment, anger, or fear to change at this stage of the game. But we can only transcend these inner structures of conditioned fear and judgment by respecting them, by working with them and letting them work with us the same way that musicians have to learn to play scales before they can play jazz. Maybe if we regard these private intimidations simply as colors and stop trying to deny them or stuff them or kill them off, we can make friends with them, with ourselves in our uniqueness and unpredictability. If we're willing, even experimentally, to put comfort, safety, and looking good aside, to refuse in ourselves anything unfriendly or heavy-handed, maybe we can trade some of our sense of original sin for a sense of original innocence and discover a newfound creativity and heroism and knack for adventure.

The paper is before us; the colors are at hand. We have this moment to find out what it feels like to put our fingers to the paint and start playing a game of follow-the-leader with our own spirit. Maybe by diving right in, by doing it *our* way, we'll learn how to laugh and play and keep following the inner friend even when we have to pee and there's not a bathroom or a bush in sight.

We can see that painting is a metaphor for the psyche's creative power; losing and finding are metaphors for the psyche's lessons; masculine and feminine are metaphors for the psyche's dual nature; sex is a metaphor for a deeper kind of union. Sometimes, I think everything is a metaphor, and that because we forget this, we wander in mazes of distraction that have nothing to do with the reality of our brief time here. That's a waste. Especially in love, we tend to confuse the symbol with the psychic truth it expresses—to get all tied up with being right, with netting this or that imagined future, with cutting someone out of our life or roping someone in. Like a mapmaker who gets so lost in his drawings that he forgets the territory that maps represent, or a composer for whom writing is more dots on a sheet of paper than inchoate sound, we mistake the metaphor for the moment, the interpretation for the thing interpreted. Denied, unrecognized, our metaphors become unconscious agendas we spread onto the world. And we lose the living quality of whatever comes forth to meet us—the slow metronome of pines swaying to the wind, the melancholy resignation of an adagio passage, the look of expectation in our lover's eyes. And if these realities— which are not our stories about them, not our judgments or plans or opinions—if these realities aren't among the colors on our palette, then what are we painting with? And what are we creating?

Mirrors and Doorways

It is not necessary to understand
the opening of the door
to feel the wind.

—Michael Luciano Ventura

 *When I was growing up in New York, my mother used to take my brother and sister and me into Manhattan where, as soon as we could, we'd make a break for the revolving door of the nearest hotel or bank. It was the ultimate thrill to push that massive booth around in its cylindrical hull, squealing at each other through the glass panels while preempted adults waited for my mother to seize control of the revolution. Imagine how easy that was—snatching three whirling dervishes out of a centrifuge on full throttle. But as we got older, she got back at us by serving up a mind-numbing, revolving-door logic that earned her a kind of upside-down admiration in the family; no one else among us could manage such dizzying philosophical observations impromptu: "He comes from a family on both sides," "In the first place, you don't even want to go in the first place; and in the second place, they don't want you along in the third*

place," and "Well, that was given a lot of too much to do about the times" are just a few examples of the jujitsu that my mother could use to swing you around and send you flying back the way you came before you knew what happened. She learned such incantations from her mother, who, one day when we were children, walked into the room where we were reading and said, "Why do you got that light shining in your eyes so's you couldn't exist?" Now, the heat source under this popcorn logic was a deeply engrained system of fears and superstitions, an irrational, mystical view of things that explained life far more powerfully than reason ever could. When the world is magical and mysterious, logical clarity isn't that important. My mother inherited this system largely intact from the Old World, shaded, of course, with the nuances of her formidable personality.

In college, I was trained to play by Aristotle's rules, not Mildred's, but long before college, my mind had been shaped by Mildred's rules, not Aristotle's. And there was just no way to get a syllogism out of "that was given a lot of too much to do about the times." Like a cold front ramming a thermal, the clash of logic and magic generated so much turbulence in my head that I couldn't be sure where I'd come out on a given issue. These two forces wrestled within me, like Jacob and the angel, vying for jurisdiction, and it would have felt a lot like racing around in the big, brass-handled bank doors of my childhood except that the fun was missing, and in its place were pitchfork jabs of high anxiety. The superstitions that still lived in the mud-tunnels of my psyche reached up through the surface whenever they could, bending rational explanation the way water bends a ray of light, while, conversely, reason sought at every turn to expose this subterranean gaggle for what it was—a disreputable clan of ignorant malingerers from a time long ago. And there I found myself, going around and *around in a revolving door between two, equally uncharitable worlds—one earthy, visceral, emotionally rich but also dark, cryptic, and unstable; the other, the world of reason, beautifully ordered and predictable but myopic and often heartless. The harder I pushed for a reconciliation between them, the faster around I went. Sometimes I seemed to live in both worlds simultaneously. For example, I considered myself a rationalist, yet before throwing out a piece of stale bread, I felt compelled to kiss it and hold it heavenward for a moment lest the gods think I was treating the spirit of nourishment with contempt. And although I believed cause and effect to be the universal glue of the cosmos, I couldn't bring myself to leave shoes on the table or a hat on the bed because I still feared what I'd been taught to fear as a child, that these acts tempted some unspeakable fate to come into the house.*

Then, one day, it hit me that these two incongruous worlds had something important in common: They were both so unfriendly that it was impossible to feel at home in either. It made little difference whether reason or superstition fired the shots—either way, the path led through enemy territory. Both worlds engaged the self antagonistically; both demanded combat-readiness. So, the choice between them wasn't a choice at all but a distraction, a magician's force—pick this ace of spades or that one. Transcendence of the conflict, then, could never come through an effort to reconcile one with the other. No, the only way out was to opt for a different view—a view based not on suspicion and self-defense but on friendship and faith in the unfolding of events. That *would be the real* revolution . . .

Mirrors have always fascinated me, especially after I began studying philosophy and found out that the most powerful and moving philosophical questions about the world are really self-questions—that is, they throw the thinker back toward his own consciousness the way a mirror throws a reflection back toward its source.

The first thing I learned about mirrors was that magicians could use them to fool people. The second thing I learned was that you have to cover the mirrors in the house when somebody in the family dies. It seems that in the old world of my peasant grandparents—the world of the shtetl, where the spirits could suddenly possess the most ordinary objects—a mirror was believed to be a doorway to the beyond. Just after a death, when the beyond was felt to be particularly close, there was a danger of slipping through this doorway. A sheet or blanket draped over the glass neutralized the magnetic pull that a mirror might exert on an unsuspecting mourner and kept the living and the dead in their respective worlds where they belonged.

Silly peasants. What did they know? Sure, Alice strayed through the looking glass into another world, but that's just make-believe. And the idea that a "mirror, mirror on the wall" can conjure apparitional images of the past and future or provide wise counsel is a fairy tale. Kid stuff. The grown-up truth is that mirrors are for shaving or putting on lipstick, and if you *should* ever happen to go through one, you might well wind up in the realm of the dead, not because a mirror is a doorway but precisely because it isn't. Or is it?

In Jean Cocteau's classic film *Orpheus,* mirrors are doorways to hell. According to Heurbetise, one of the story's main characters: "Mirrors are the doors through which death comes and goes. Look at yourself in a mirror all your life and you'll see death at work." The film itself seems to mirror Cocteau's vision of postwar intellectual France as self-important, fickle, and vacuous—and one can hardly miss the imagery. Mirrors are ego, and ego is the threshold to a world of isolation, suffering, judgment, and swift punishment. Now, I've performed as a musician, danced lead roles in hundreds of stage productions, and put on a pretty good show in one way or another most of my life, and I know how damning the concern over appearances can be. It can take you right out of your body, right out of who you are. You start living inside out, living in the mirror. And then where are you?

But there's another way to move through a mirror. To understand it, we'll need to take a closer look at this business about "throwing consciousness back on itself." The philosophers in the audience will recognize this idea as shorthand for Hegel's famous dialectic of consciousness, which most of us were introduced to in school. Remember? Thesis + Antithesis = Synthesis. Or, in plain English: Something happens, something contradicts it, something else happens as a result. This "something else" then becomes the new thesis, and the process repeats, *ad* the same sort of *infinitum* that you see when you place two mirrors face to face. So far, so good.

Now, if you look a little deeper into the glass, you discover that the dialectic is really a bit trickier than that because it involves a kind of switch-a-rooney: You see, the synthesis isn't just a *compromise* between two opposing forces but actually a new slant that resolves the conflict, oddly enough, by showing that there never really was a conflict to begin with. In this "sublation," as Hegel called it, the so-called conflict is revealed to have been merely the *appearance* of a conflict, and presto—the seeming conflict is "resolved."

We have to be careful here. Mirrors are symbols of the truth—they reflect whatever is set before them—but we mustn't forget that they're also used by magicians to fool people. If you ever went to Palisades Amusement Park or Coney Island in their day, you know how lost you can get wandering around in a hall of mirrors—the little hell of not being able to find a real doorway anywhere. And it's even easier to get lost wandering around in the mirrored halls of philosophical thought. Before you know it, you can stumble through an opening, and there you are, not quite among the living. So, to play it safe, we'd better cover the mirror of blinding theoretical thought with the cloth of a practical illustration.

It's a Wednesday afternoon, and I'm talking to Rick about a fizzling relationship, spinning my mental wheels in a ditch, when he suddenly asks me what I'm feeling. "Feeling?" I say. "Well, I guess I feel that I should try to work this thing out because she's really a good person and—" "Hold on," Rick says. "What are you *feeling*?" "Uh—I feel, uh, that—I—uh, really don't want to—hurt anybody and that I should be able to make this thing work because—" Rick shakes his head, not buying any of it. "Look, I'm *telling* you what I feel," I say indignantly. "No you're not," says Rick. "Feelings are *simple*. Happy, sad, angry, scared—sensations any five-year-old can have if his psyche hasn't been taken to the cleaners. So, pretend you're five and tell me what you're feeling." There's a pause while the dialectical arrow thwacks a bull's-eye. "I feel scared," I say quietly. "And a little sad. And confused." "Yeah," Rick says. "Maybe instead of figuring it all out, you can just sit with that for a while."

The unexamined thesis I had carried for as long as I could remember—that complex thoughts, judgments, fantasies, and conclusions are feelings—was thrown back on itself when Rick held up the mirror of a more intuitively convincing antithesis—that what I was describing couldn't be my feelings, because feelings are simple. An unnerving inner conflict followed: I'm having all these complicated feelings, but feelings aren't complicated. How can I be feeling feelings that aren't feelings? They feel like feelings. But if they're not feelings, what are they? For a moment, I felt paralyzed. But when I deferred to the greater truth of Rick's point, I suddenly experienced a liberating *synthesis*—that the mental reflections I had taken to be my feelings not only weren't my feelings but never had been. In fact, without realizing it, I had been using the word *feel* in a way that actually inhibited emotional sensation, reinforcing the thesis, which Rick had brought into question for the first time. The synthesis freed me to feel physically—in my stomach, heart, throat, face, and hands— the simple emotions that had been stashed behind the locked door of unexamined belief in a false image. As this door opened and a new angle of vision came into focus, the unsettling conflict of a few moments before disappeared like breath on a mirror.

Dialectical resolution shows you that what you thought you knew, you only *thought* you knew, essentially altering your present, your probable future, and even your past in a flash and transporting you into an integrity that couldn't have been imagined in the earlier terms—a "beyond" of sorts. The final irony in this revealing-through-reversing is that as our psyche evolves, we become transformed increasingly into who we already are. So, the "beyond" turns out to be right here. In becoming more self-aware, our psyche passes through the dialectical mirror into a larger room with a bigger view, a room in which we can apprehend ourselves and the world with greater clarity. From this larger room, we can see that, although we thought we *were* being ourselves, we were really only living in reflections. The new grounding is thus provided, and like magic, we've moved through to a greater present. Call this synthesis. Or learning. Or rebirth. Or personal transformation. Whatever the label, it seems that my peasant grandparents were right. Mirrors *can* be doorways to the beyond.

In this sense, the Sunset Grill is, physically, a living metaphor of personal evolution. All the ingredients of synthesis are there: nourishment, openness, accommodation, and big windows letting in lots of light. So, it's probably no accident that we picked the Grill as the place we would meet and hold up mirrors for each other to pass through.

Friends help you see where you are by loving you *as you are,* and by telling you the truth, even when you're being crazy—*especially* then. And although facing the truth may be uncomfortable, whatever willingness there is in you to step through the mirror to greater life will listen and consider. Now, this friendly counsel isn't exactly cultivated by the prevailing forces of relativity and consumerism. After all, who can say who's crazy? Why should we trust our friends' "opinions" of us more than our own conclusions? And why should friendship, of all things, make us uncomfortable? Aren't we *entitled* to be comfortable? We're *Americans*. That makes it our spiritual duty to be individuals, to finger paint our way right into Manifest Destiny, from sea to shining sea, with liberty and justice for all. On one hand, we have the traditions of laissez-faire capitalism and personal freedom pushing us into our separate selves. On the other hand, there's been a brushfire resurgence of entrepreneurship and self-employment across the country that has seen people trading the corporate/bureaucratic/alienating-but-still-social workplace for living room offices where the only way to reach out and touch someone else is through the latest electronics—computer, phone, and fax. So, the major, grass-roots decentralization of the workplace has produced a corresponding increase in the number of people earning their living each day in relative isolation. As if this weren't enough to cut us off from each other, we're also bombarded by the ultimate edict of advertising: Worship appearances. If we look like this, smell like this, dress like this, drive this car, exercise in this health club, we'll be fulfilled human beings. We can even use a 900-number to direct-dial "love," which, if you ask me, shows just how far the gloves have come off. I figure we're about two years from throwing street people to the lions. Maybe we already have.

The more we practice living in isolation, the less likely we are to take part in real dialogue with other people, and this can quickly place us in the dangerous position of the characters in *Orpheus*—lost in our own reflections. When we forsake our *outer* mirrors, we have no place to go for a little distance and perspective and honest reflection. In the face of steamrolling "individuality," a pervasive climate of competition, fixation on appearances, withdrawal from the social workplace, and rampant consumerism, the mirror becomes a portal leading straight to hell, to a world without doorways, a world in which the fires of the thesis-without-antithesis consume *us*. A society that encourages this emotional and psychic isolation teaches us to avoid the reflections that might change us. Fortunately, all we need to reclaim what these forces would take away, is each other, and the willingness to see what's right in front of us.

Real friendship is not collusion, not two people sitting in a cafe with no intention of seeing something more, each half-listening to the other's monologue—in effect, two mirrors facing away from each other. What's missing there is the possibility of antithesis—the reflection of one in the other, and so, the doorway. Because real friendship involves the risk of psychic change, it can be unsettling, even disturbing. There are labor pains, rites of passage, periods of acclimation. It isn't easy to change worlds. Watch someone being born or dying, and you'll see how we're all drawn, pushed, or dragged through doorways, often kicking and screaming. Even starting a new job or moving to a different city can be murder. Sometimes there are no words, and all you can do is wait it out together until the new order settles into place. But this is how it is with friends. Honesty holds up the mirror, a doorway opens, and the love gets you through.

We live in the midst of outer forces as well as inner ones, and we can only bring all of this together in the fullness of our identity by making friends with whatever's trying to work itself out in our relationships. Finger painting *is* the starting point; we begin by honoring the creative impulses of our inner life, but never to the exclusion of the outer one. At some point, the whole inner/outer distinction runs into an antithesis of its own and gets recast in the light of a greater whole in which one understands that there never was an inner or an outer in the first place, but only life reflecting life. Until we see this, we might make the mistake of using notions such as "individuality," "personal freedom," and "intuition"—all of which have their validity—to avoid the fundamental change that comes from looking in the mirror of the world. Finger painting is the beginning, but once we come out of our hiding places and show ourselves to even one other person, once we become willing to see ourselves reflected in a different light, *we* become the paint, and the greater hands of friendship, of the spirit's opening and closing doors, of timing and the beyond, can draw us in and create something with *us*.

You can explore these doorways by meeting a friend and telling him something that you've felt you had to keep secret. Maybe something you want but consider too silly to talk about. Or something that's been weighing on you and resisting resolution—a recurring dream or a long-held fear, nagging feelings about your work, doubts about your marriage, worry over an affair you had. Be reasonably sure that the friend you choose to be your mirror *is* a friend, someone you trust and respect, someone who can listen without judging, without giving advice, who can be a calm, reflecting surface. Then do it—call him, meet with him, open yourself up and tell him, face to face. What you find on the other side of this opening may surprise you. There's always more than meets the eye, always bigger rooms waiting to receive us just on the other side of the mirrors of friendship.

"We're the prisoners of the secrets we keep," says a wise adage; still it's difficult to come out of hiding and change long-practiced ways, even when they no longer serve us. It takes courage and a greater interest in looking in the mirror than in looking good. But there are some journeys we can only make together. We need the doorways that mirrors become when we're willing to stand naked before them. And one more thing: Remember to offer thanks in the direction of the Old World before stepping through into the new one. My Russian grandmother would be proud of you.

When Kären was promoted to senior editor at Central Florida Magazine, *we went out to dinner at the Grill to celebrate. After a few coffees, we were feeling ready for something more, so we got in my car and went whizzing down Highway 436 with the sunroof open. Suddenly, she said, "He lives pretty close to here." "Who?" I asked, knowing the answer. "Him," she said—the guy who left her, the guy she still hadn't been able to leave. In a few minutes, she indicated an apartment complex on the right and said wistfully, "There. He lives in there." So, slave to protocol that I am, I squealed into the complex while Kären watched with shifting expressions of horror and delight. "Where?" I demanded, "Which building?" She pointed out a second-story apartment, and as I pulled up, we could see the soft, orange glow of a living room through the sliding glass doors of the balcony. Stopping the car right out in front, I stood up through the sunroof and yelled, "Jerk! You could have had this incredible woman! You could have had her!" As I did this, Kären was trying desperately to drag me back down into the car, but it was all she could do to breathe. Finally, she managed to pull me into my seat, and we sped away. A mile or so down the road, she was still gasping for air, laughing wildly and stamping her feet, and her mascara had run so badly that she looked like a raccoon. Then things gradually settled down, and the car grew quiet for a time as we drove back to Kären's place. When I dropped her off, she said, "I haven't felt this good in years." It was a nutty thing to do, but it brought the lofty image she'd been carrying of this man back down to earth and made it a bit more manageable.*

The loss of love can spark war in the psyche, a war of attrition in which maudlin romanticism and flights of self-pity can starve you out. In fighting such a war, sometimes nonsense is the better part of valor.

Heaven and Earth

So you must not be frightened . . . if a sadness rises
up before you larger than any you have ever seen;
if a restiveness, like light and cloud-shadows,
passes over your hands and over all you do. You
must think that something is happening with you,
that life has not forgotten you, that it holds you in
its hand; it will not let you fall.

> —Rainer Maria Rilke
> *Letters to a Young Poet*

 *In April 1990, I flew out to San Fran-
cisco for the wedding of my friends
Norman Hering and Patti McKay. The
big earthquake on October 17, only six
months earlier, had demolished the Marina, the Cypress over-
pass, and other hapless targets in the city, and seismograph
needles were still twitching fretfully, recording hundreds of
aftershocks each week. I remember thinking en route, "I hope
there's a quake while I'm out here this time. Nothing big
enough to hurt anybody—just a harmless shudder or two so
I can see what it's like." During the week I was there, two
small quakes—one of them registering 4.5—did hit the Bay
Area, sending some nasty tremors and bad vibes through the
building I was in and making front-page headlines the next
day. Fortunately, no one was hurt, and there wasn't any real
damage.*

But there's another earthquake going on all the time in San Francisco, a social one. Its epicenter is in the area around Market and Powell, where the casualties hang out. After walking there for a while, I detoured into a store to pick up a couple of sandwiches and some french fries and was soon back on the street. In a few minutes, I passed by a heavyset man sitting on a red brick planter that housed a healthy spray of flowers. He was stopping people halfheartedly to see if they would give him "anything, anything at all," so I went over and asked if he was hungry. Beside him sat a bearded man wearing a cowboy hat with the brim pulled low and a rope tie with a turquoise-stone pull; his face was burlap—in better days, he might have presided over an Indian tribal council. The other guy said yeah, he was hungry, so I gave him the bag of food, but as I handed it over, for a few seconds—maybe four or five, which can be a long time—his eyes locked on mine like radar, and we smiled. The Indian, watching the transaction, nodded once with unmistakable dignity. And we all understood, at least momentarily, that the problem is enormous, that one sandwich makes absolutely no difference and at the same time, makes all the difference there is, because it draws a line between being fed and being hungry, between feeling that somebody gives a damn and feeling that you're on your own in the rubble of a society that takes better care of its street plants than its street people.

By the third day, hanging out in the earthquake zone had put me off, and I began to feel a familiar rumble of anxiety. So, I got on the J Church Muni for a ride back to Noe Valley where I figured I'd take a reassuring middle-class stroll along hilly sidewalks lined with redundant chiropractic clinics, nail salons, and coffee boutiques. As I stepped up onto the Muni, the driver eyed me.

"How much?" I asked nervously.

"Eighty-five cents," he grinned, "if you don't ask for directions."

"How much if I do?" I asked, amused.

"Same," he said.

He smiled, and I saw that he had no teeth. We nodded at each other as though we were old friends; then, I put some coins into the fare box and took a seat. As the Muni eased out, I looked through the back window at where I'd come from and noticed the fog falling softly over the hills of the city.

I hate being up in the air. It's always the same. Even before we taxi onto the runway, I start trying to engage the reluctant stranger next to me in nervous conversation about the wonder of flight. There I sit, all buckled in, chair and tray in the full upright position, doing my best to comprehend that this behemoth of metal and gadgetry, this cross between a tank and a Greyhound bus, in a matter of seconds, will accelerate with unnerving speed to about 140 miles per hour, then suddenly, with a slight backward pull on its high-tech reins, will climb *up* through thin air to an altitude of some thirty thousand feet. And there it will cruise with me, a modern Jonah, in its belly, along with the mumbling businessman beside me using his attache case for a desk; the old, gray-haired black man in the green bow tie one row aft; the gurgling infant two rows fore; and all these others—too many of us, too much weight for a safe takeoff, I'm sure of it. Time and circumstance have brought us together for this cross-country vault over busy cities, mighty mountains, and patchwork farmland, and now, here we sit, belted in and ready to rock and roll over six and a half miles of icy free-fall.

I take a deep breath and relax into the ride as the engines thrust us down the runway. And then, we angle upward, off the earth. Watching cloud-steam blasting back over the wings, I suddenly think of Rilke. Takeoff is the most dangerous part, so I look for a ready distraction and notice that the flight attendant has a beautiful, long neck that turns gracefully as she mimes her way through the here's-how-you-buckle-your-seatbelt routine for the ten-thousandth time. Soon, we level out. A muted bell sounds. The captain turns off the no-smoking sign. We're on our way, and if there's no turbulence, we won't even have as much sensation of movement as you get riding in the back of an Airstream travel trailer on the interstate. Just twelve uneasy naps, three hundred imaginary disasters, four magazines, and one connecting flight later, the cap'n (God, please don't let him be an alcoholic) will put this baby down on a runway at the San Francisco airport. So does the technology of flying allow us to bend space and time to our will and arrive on the other side of the country before lunch.

Between taxi and takeoff, several images come spinning out of my mind like a bunch of Shriners in those idiotic minicars, doing wheelies and nearly bashing into each other. In one, the guy in the back who resembles Bill Bixby turns out to be a terrorist. In another, something in the baggage hold that looks a lot like plastic explosive wired to a clock suddenly stops ticking. As these images fade, I survey the ceiling of the cabin and wonder if this plane has gone up and down once too often, expanding and contracting like a balloon the way they do, and if at thirty-five thousand feet, the roof is suddenly going to turn to shredded wheat.

Okay, this seems like a good time to take a break from the doom thinking and tell you a little about my house. It's a cute two-bedroom built in 1956, with all the idiosyncrasies of post-Korea residential design, including two-pronged (read "ungrounded") electrical outlets. Now, ungrounded outlets can be hazardous to the health of a computer, laser printer, answering machine, cordless phone, and various other electronic gizmos that I bought because I really needed them to do my work and not just because they're neat, so I scheduled an appointment with an electrician. We'll call her Paula, because that's her name. Paula told me all about electricity and why you should never use one of those little three-to-two prong adaptors. Seems that, in your basic ungrounded outlet, a few electrons can go berserk and start partying inside the guts of your hypersensitive, state-of-the-art equipment. Once they're out of the chute, these microphysical renegades, like the free particles in a uranium critical mass, can tear through circuitry like 20-gauge buckshot. By grounding the outlet—that is, by running a wire from the outlet box to an eight-foot pole that gets pounded into the ground—you give these tiny Tasmanian devils a path that leads away from the hardware. So, grounding is our friend.

Now, grounding is just as important for human beings as it is for computers because thoughts and feelings, like electrons, frequently leap off the straight-and-narrow and head for parts unknown within the human psyche, ripping their way as they go and producing short-circuits, deadlocks, and feedback loops that take us way off course. Getting grounded means returning our awareness to the present, here, now, without a mental or emotional agenda. We take a deep breath, get quiet, open ourselves, become receptive, attentive, intelligently aware instead of spinning in a Shriner car of runaway thought or emotion. We have our feet firmly on the ground of the present, so we have a solid sense of who we are and where we stand.

I learned that people can be as grounded or ungrounded as

electrical outlets from Jean Mezera, who, in addition to being well grounded herself, is a codependency and addictions counselor with a practice in Maitland, Florida. We were talking one day, and I was, as usual, flying around the room— eyes, mind, and tongue racing well ahead of reality. Jean let this go on for a bit, then said: "Do you realize how ungrounded you are?" "What?" I said, offended. "Me? Ungrounded? Hey, I'm as grounded as the next guy. What do you mean by *grounded?*" "You're not grounded, and you know what I mean," Jean said matter-of-factly. Again, I protested. The silence grew silenter. Then, Jean asked, "Is Joe grounded?" referring to a common friend of ours. I sat still until a feeling for Joe arrived in my heart and gut. "No," I said, "Joe isn't grounded." "And Lynn?" Jean asked. "No way," I said, without hesitation. "And Mike?" "Sometimes. Sometimes he's grounded." "Right," said Jean. "How about me?" she asked, placing her fingers against her chest. "Yes," I said quietly, "you're grounded." Finally, she pointed at me. "And you?" she said. Again, I sat quietly with the question until the present came into focus. "No," I admitted, "I'm not grounded." So, Jean was right—I did know. But as long as I was busy being ungrounded, I didn't know what I knew. Finding out what we know is one thing that happens when we get grounded.

Now the last time I flew, something different happened. At first, the takeoff evoked the usual inventory of imaginary catastrophes: I heard an engine choke up, felt a sudden loss of power, and saw a gremlin on the wing trying to peel back the cowling just as it did in the original "Twilight Zone" episode, "Nightmare at 20,000 Feet," based on Richard Matheson's short story and featuring a great performance by William Shatner. Anyway, instead of gritting my teeth and toughing it out, I decided to let go, to make room in my awareness for everything I was thinking and feeling. I simply kicked back and watched the whole show of self—the imaginings, the fear, the shallow breathing, the endlessly repeating anticipation of some dreaded "it." This unconditional self-witnessing was mind-blowing, a paradox, because it involved grounding myself in the very present in which I was being ungrounded. So, my awareness circled back and reclaimed itself exactly as it was, while logic and reason took a much-needed snooze. By cooperating with the moment rather than fighting it, I made room for something new to show itself, and it did, because I suddenly began to experience the *safety* of flying. I could feel how much the plane wanted to stay aloft, that its nature, its very essence, was flight, and I began to feel more ensconced in the plane than abducted by it. The cloudscapes, whose beauty and presence had been submerged by uneasy preoccupations, now broke through the surface of my awareness like dolphins sounding playfully. Note that I didn't *try* to relax or make myself enjoy the flight. I didn't tell myself that I shouldn't be nervous, that flying is the safest form of transportation, and yada, yada, yada. All I did was stop resisting my own physical and emotional sensations and set up a friendly connection with them, a ground wire. This unresisting awareness of the moment exactly as it is grounds us in the present and keeps us from taking off into flights of fancy that don't serve us, no matter how much our habits, fears, or desires are trying to stuff a boarding pass into our hands.

As with electricity, there are two currents that flow through the human psyche—the "to be" and "not to be" that charge every situation with the essential either/or, the primal choice that Camus considered the only important one, namely, whether or not to commit suicide. This is, of course, also the question of whether to live or merely exist. We can focus on

"Yes, we're going to die, but we're alive!" or, "Yes, we're alive, but we're going to die!" And here, "Which came first?" is more than a riddle about a chicken or an egg because in both cases, the timid little word *but* takes the first part of the statement hostage and hijacks us to the second, stealing back what was just granted and giving us the bum's rush straight through the door of the opposite conclusion. After the last part of the sentence, we're left with a feeling that the first part didn't really count. "I'd love to quit this job and start my own company, *but I'd have to be crazy to give up the security.*" "I wish I could be closer to my child, *but we're both so busy.*" "I'd like to ask her out, *but I don't want to risk the rejection.*" Always after this word *but* comes the excuse, the alibi that keeps us hung up precisely because it conceals our often formidable loyalty to preventing the very thing that we claim we want. "I wish I could be closer to my child, but we're both so busy." You will take off on this logic only if you have a commitment to emotional distance, despite the first part of the sentence. Certainly, you and your child may have busy schedules, but closeness is a way of being, not something else to jot down on an already crowded list of things to do. Parents don't get close to their children by having lots of leisure time but rather by making a decision not to let anything else pre-empt thirty seconds of eye contact, a generous hug, and a few minutes of attentive listening each day. The parent who believes that he and his child are too busy to be close is not yet grounded in the truth of his predicament, which will only show itself to him when he can see the alibi for what it is. It's not that he can't be close because he's too busy, but that he stays too busy because he chooses not to be close. The polarity of our choices is often reversed.

There is, of course, pain in not being close to one's child, or one's lover, as there is in a great many of the things that we unwittingly choose, and here we may wonder why someone would elect to stay in pain, especially when another voice in his psyche is calling out for the end of that pain. This may be because he associates a greater pain with giving it up, and this reveals something startling: Every decision "to be" is also a decision "not to be," every gain, a loss. To enjoy the airplane flight, one has to say good-bye to one's old traveling companions, hypervigilance and crisis planning. To get married, one must divorce the single life and some of the ease, simplicity, and comfort of solitude. To have a child, one must begin to walk irrevocably away from one's own childhood. And this explains how we can tenaciously cling to our old ways even while wanting to be done with them once and for all. We're not ready to face the sadness of the good-bye, or the anxiety of a future without the self we've always been.

The most amazing thing about having a child is how time accelerates. The first fifteen years of a human life are stage to an ongoing metamorphosis that makes caterpillar-into-butterfly magic look like a parlor trick. Along the racing continuum of time that came into the world with my daughter, an infant became a baby and the baby, somehow, a little girl; the little girl transformed into a teenager, the teenager into a young woman. There were no rites of passage, no points along the way where we stopped and said good-bye to all the people she had been and all the people I had been, correspondingly. The members of this fading family procession were precious, irreplaceable, and they left as mysteriously as they appeared, but we were far too busy being them, too busy becoming them to recognize that they had come and gone and that we had lost them. So, we moved forward into the next and the next and the next in turn with only a dream-sense of the losses that trailed silently behind, like the wake of movement left in the air by a dancer's arm. Maybe this is why even the happiest changes in our life often leave us feeling oddly sad, confused, or ambivalent: Every step taken is a step left behind—every beginning an ending. And every ending reminds us that we live in a world where things end. It's hard enough for some of us to connect with the grief of an outright loss. How much harder to find, ground, and release the grief hiding in the victory, to pierce the psychic armor of one-sidedness and honor that pain, too? Who takes the time to do that? And yet, our ability to be, to live fully, may depend on our willingness to say good-bye when the time comes.

Still, through all the changes, all the good-byes, something endures. I can see it sometimes in my daughter's eyes when she looks at me and, suddenly, we both know, both get the joke of being alive at all. There's a grounding there, and a joy too tiny to talk about. What endures is the earthy present—rich, full, self-sufficient, the present in which, as Rilke wrote, life holds us in its hands and will not let us fall. Or as G. K. Chesterton put it, frogs not only jump—they seem to *like* to. Even so, they don't stay in the air long, and we will do well to follow their example. At some point, we need to learn how to land where we are, to feel what's under our feet and how things stand with us. It's best not to postpone this too long. We don't have forever, and the earth is a wonderful place to be if we can only get here while there's time.

For years, the members of the Grill society have been aware that the friendship we share is probably also the best foundation for two people "in love." This friendship has been grounded in trust, emotional honesty, respect for each other's right to choose, and a commitment to support our individual spiritual development and well-being.

Because we aren't in love with each other, aren't romanti-

cally or sexually involved within the group, the friendship formula has been pretty simple and easy to maintain. We've talked for years about how transplantable this grounding might be to a relationship that includes the additional dimensions of in-loveness, and have hoped for the best while waiting for time, destiny, luck, or whatever to arrange the necessary meeting. And we've wondered how much the old wrestle-and-rope-'em, rodeo approach to courtship had been tempered by our evolution together and emotional recovery from inherited and long-practiced patterns. Most of us weren't going to have to wait long to find out.

COURTSHIP

"Won't you let me go with you?"
"Yes, my love, yes!"

—Peter Yarrow
"The Cruel War Is Raging"

Hot Pursuit

Madam . . . I wish you'd keep my hands to yourself.

—Groucho Marx
Monkey Business

 *The other day, while taking a brisk constitutional through Winter Park, I noticed that I wasn't just walking—I was pushing myself through space, exerting far more effort than was needed to put one foot in front of the other and cover ground. This came as a surprise, and reminded me of advice I've heard all my life from teachers and friends, parents, partners, even from my daughter: "You're trying too hard. Relax. Do less."*

As I eased back on the throttle, slowing my pace, my breathing softened, and it seemed as though the sky, the trees, the sidewalk all came into sharper focus. I realized that rushing is a way of being ahead of yourself, of missing the moment. And I thought of how much I had rushed ahead in matters of the heart. Hadn't I too often missed the people I loved, even while with them? Wasn't there an odd, self-perpetuating loneliness in this excessive effort?

Dennis's philosophy is that it's all a gift. Making it through 1986, he says, brought him a second chance, and he's grateful for whatever goodness comes along. No more grasping, no more rushing ahead. I think about how little I've been able to embody this wisdom. Love still seems so urgent sometimes, so likely to fall into dust in the next moment, so undependable. Death is, after all, always just a breath away—it's only a matter of which breath—and by walking a little faster, might we not slip past death the way children playing tag slip past the one who's It, the one who, with a touch, can snuff them out of the game? Death pulls us to a hurrying, and as if this weren't enough, our losses push us from behind, as though if we can just go fast enough, we can keep from feeling them and prevent their recurrence.

How to trust time, the world, other people? How to slow down? How to let in the trees and the sky and love again, with soft breath and clear vision? How to make room for oneself to live in the face of the urgency to live while there's time? How to make room for another?

When it comes to courtship, I've always relied on the Hot Pursuit Method: First you get hot, then you pursue. Usually, the next step for me has been to propose marriage as soon as possible. This always seemed like the perfectly obvious thing to do; I mean, it even *felt* right. Now, transactional analysts, the therapists who like to draw those stacked Parent-Adult-Child circles and figure out who's talking to whom in a given conversation, would call this sort of courtship behavior *scripty*. This means that it smacks of early parental programming, something along the lines of: "If you're attracted to her, you must love her; if you love her, you must marry her." Buried deep in the psyche, a curse such as this compels you to find somebody willing to read corresponding lines from the same script, and there you are: meeting, getting hot, pursuing, and marrying, only to eventually find yourself cooled down, divorced, alone, numb, and without a clue.

In reviewing our courtship experiences, the members of the Sunset Grill society found a common theme: We had always been in a big hurry—to get "involved," to get into bed, to get to the altar, to get *somewhere*. There were warning shots— inner admonitions to slow down, but we typically ignored them, preferring in the heat of the moment to proceed at full tilt. I came to think of this as the ability to go "faster than the truth," and noticed that each of us had his own way of putting another log on the fire: Kären flashed her eyes a lot. Rick liked to take over, drive the car from the passenger's seat. Gretchen had a blend of earth-mother/social activist that was damned near irresistible. Dennis turned into a cocker spaniel. As for me, I liked to self-preen, twirl my back locks while sending out waves of boyish insouciance. Like the man said, the secret to acting is honesty—when you can fake that, you've got it made.

Not that we were the only ones displaying oddly colored feathers. Some of the women I was with turned into babies as soon as we entered the courtship arena, complete with puzzled looks, lip-biting, and knock-kneed posturing. Others turned into my mother. One turned into Stalin. But the beauty of courtship is a kind of Midas touch that transforms even the most hideous flaw into the pure gold of an adorable idiosyncrasy, so it was never hard to keep the game going and reality at bay. She's not demanding, she's *enthusiastic;* he isn't stubborn, he's *persistent;* she's not childish, she's *spontaneous.* We lived within these dreams, and they were real for us until we woke up with the pieces falling from our hands like a shattered mirror, which in a way, they were. Then, courtship seemed little more than a delightful ritual of collusion in which two people get together so that each can create the other in the image of his or her own desires. Our "love" had once again run its course like a flu, and we found ourselves face to face with an actual *person* who suddenly had many flaws that now refused to be cute: the knight in shining armor turned out to be a guy who peed around the toilet; the princess became a ruthless adolescent with a shoe fetish; Brando, Redford, and Newman changed into Larry, Moe, and Curly right before our eyes. It was horrible, not what we'd bargained for at all. But was this plunge back to earth from the lofty heights of romantic fervor due to some lack of forthrightness on our part, or was it inherent in courtship itself?

The crux of the matter seemed to be this "faster than the truth" business. When we looked at this closely, we found two things: First, we'd all grown up in an age that worshiped speed, that made it the very framework of gratification—casual sex, fast food, credit cards, telecommunications, air travel, personal computers—the faster the better. Second, we were in a hurry because we felt *needy*. Somehow, we'd all arrived at the cast-iron conviction that love wasn't going to be there for us, that it couldn't be trusted, that we didn't deserve to be loved or even have needs—never mind having them met. We had lived for as long as we could remember in this narcissistic self-denial, and now, in mid-life, we were starving. When love's feast was set before us, how could we go slowly?

Peeling back another layer, we saw that this sense of urgency was by no means limited to our courtship activities. In fact, we were running most of the time—when we talked, when we worked, behind the steering wheel, at the dinner table—even when we were just sitting around doing nothing, inside we were barreling along at escape velocity, hurtling away from a simple grounding in the living present, our minds racing, expectations and assumptions in full mutiny. It was as though we were caught in a mad game of psychic tag—we had to avoid being It, and we could do that only by making somebody else It. Now, *It* is whatever fires up your zest for life, whatever anchors and rejuvenates you and gives your existence direction and meaning. We had all come to believe that this It was "out there" somewhere rather than a condition of our own psyche. In living this belief, we continually projected our own power, gave it away to the world, to circumstances, to our partners—in fact, to just about everybody and everything that came along, which is why we became emotional hostages if someone so much as looked at us crooked. Any driver who swore at us from a passing car could have our power, any salesclerk who'd had a hard day. In fact, we found blaming others, judging others, reacting to others, and perhaps most of all, rescuing and "fixing" others every bit as irresistible as falling in love.

This obsessive disowning of power became even more tangled up in courtship, because while we were busy trying to get our partners to be It for us, they were trying to get us to be It for them. "After you . . ." "Oh, no, after you . . ." "Oh, no no no . . . after *you*." Then came the inevitable resentments, the stuffed anger, the bewilderment, the withholding, and at the end of the game, the divvying up of belongings. Having gone through this pain enough times, we finally understood that nobody can be It for anybody else. Which meant that our neediness for love, however deeply felt, was fundamentally misguided, and in this sense, false. When we were "involved," we felt fulfilled, valuable, whole; but when things got rough, when romance deferred to the demands of everyday togetherness, as it always does eventually, we became disillusioned (though unfortunately for us, not literally) and we ran, not realizing that no outer bond can do more than mirror the spiritual condition of those who enter into it. We had taken partnership to be the foundation of our inner life, whereas it's really the other way around. Finally, spent by our accumulated losses and pent-up grief, we had to stop, turn, and admit the painful, unsettling truth that most of what we had been doing with our former partners amounted to "practicing" love because we had not yet entered a loving, accepting relationship with our own psyche, and *this* was the underlying source of our emotional emptiness. It wasn't the love of another that we needed to become whole—*that* never worked for long. It was our own love that we lacked, an experience of our own, unpartnered sufficiency and worth.

Which brings us to Delton Scudder. In every life, I suppose, there are unforgettable people—characters who stand out from the commonplace and somehow remain in memory with much of the vividness and importance they had when you knew them. So it is for me with Dr. Scudder. He was a short, white-haired man, a distinguished professor with a vast understanding of Eastern philosophy. I can still see him at the front of one of the amphitheater classrooms in Little Hall, lecturing extemporaneously, stopping every few minutes to clear his throat and, from time to time, gesturing grandly as though poised on the main stage of the Metropolitan Opera House. He was chairman of the religion department at the University of Florida then, back in 1969, but he was as much a storyteller as a teacher or administrator. The class met each Monday evening for three hours while, outside, Gainesville's January winds blasted the streets and blew the Spanish moss from the live oaks. There was a feeling to that time, a charge of expectation and purpose that belonged to the cold, to the quickening of personal politics, to the Beatles' music, to the thrill of being away at college. And we were all an essential part of it—Jimi Millikan and Tom Hanna, Thaxton Springfield, Henry Allison, Austin Creel, Joel Seigel, Tina Carlton, Walter Guthrie, Charlie Jarrett, Jimi Poulos, Joy Eaton, Steve Toscar, and others who were, for me, less indelible but no less important to what was taking place. We sensed the mighty wave of change sweeping through the country, and we leaned toward it, into it the way a gull must lean into a thermal to climb surely, suddenly, into the icy blue.

One night, Dr. Scudder was reviewing a passage from the *Tao Teh Ching,* the central text of Taoism. "The sage never uses force to overcome," he said, his gravelly voice accompanied by the fluorescent hum in the room. "Force is followed by a loss of strength. This is not the Way. Whatever goes against the Way comes to an early end." Then he paused, and his eyes grew distant, as though he were looking through the back wall of the room at some ancient horizon. In a few minutes, he started rambling as he often did, this time about his wife—about pulling a chair out for her in a restaurant and how much he loved her. Like an old mime, he slid back an imaginary chair, smiling. Then he asked us what we thought it would be like to live in the world graciously, as though we were guests here . . .

I like this idea of living graciously, in a state of natural grace, and I wonder how it might be applied to courtship. Maybe if Dr. Scudder keeps reminding us from the other world, we'll eventually remember to approach our loves with the same generous doses of appreciation and kindness that good guests always show their hosts. Maybe we can learn to go slowly and pay attention to what's really there rather than go tearing off into a projection. Maybe we'll be able to be in love with each other according to the Way—naturally, gently, without effort, without resistance—and share what's neat about us more than what's needy. Maybe we can even stop hotly pursuing love long enough to sit still and *receive* it. Because in the great dance of courtship, the mad flapping of feathers is strictly for the birds.

When I was a boy, I used to go to synagogue on Saturday mornings. I was filled with magic and innocence, then, and I remember thinking that when the rabbi opened the Ark of the Covenant and the congregation sang out, the music rose up the Ark like smoke up a flue, eventually reaching heaven, where God paid loving attention to every note. I also remember that the red, electric lamp that hung in front of the Ark was called the "light eternal." And I wondered about this. How could it be? What if the electricity gets turned off? Or the bulb burns out—it has to, sooner or later? Can there really be a light that goes on and on and on?

Now, many years later, I no longer believe that our songs reached heaven. Or that a loving God is watching over us the way I believed as a child. But I still wonder if there's a light that never burns out, and secretly hope there is.

Buy a Ticket

Faith can move mountains, but not furniture.
                                    —Leo Rosten
                        The Giant Book of Laughter

 *Every so often, Kären goes to visit a woman named Sue, who's psychic. Sue has her shuffle a deck of cards, then deal them out in a row, and the reading begins. Over the years, Kären has got the same sort of information in these sessions—that she's going to meet a man who lives near the water, that her work will make her rich and celebrated, that she's on a solid spiritual path and that, consequently, her dreams are all going to come true. Now, I went to see Sue once. Twice, actually, in the interest of rational inquiry. We should be open-minded about these things, I explained to the committee of professors in my psyche who rose up in arms at the thought of my going to see a person of the psychic persuasion. Left-brain bigots. At least they'd already given me my degree, so there wasn't a whole lot they could do about it.*

Sue wasn't what I expected. She was in her eighties, nearly

blind, and as sharp as they come. Her skin was translucent with age, almost luminous. She ushered me into the back room, her big German shepherd following suspiciously beside me, and we took our seats next to a small table. As we chatted, I relaxed somewhat, though I still felt embarrassed and self-conscious about being there. The professors had gone underground, probably to organize a revolt; they can be pretty revolting. Anyway, what was on my mind at the time was my former wife, the possibility of reconciliation, and the question of a love life in general. As I shuffled the deck, I was careful not to let on that these were my thoughts.

I dealt the cards as Sue instructed, whereupon she began looking them over the way a zoology student might survey the innards of some haplessly splayed reptile. Then, in a frail voice, she started a free-associative rap that went like this: "You're too nice to be alone. You'll meet someone, a woman, slender but not short. She has a good sense of humor, likes to wisecrack, but also can be subdued. She is more spiritually compatible with you than the woman you are hurt about. She will have recently gone through the loss of a loved one, too, but her values will sustain her through this time. She sees death as a transition, as an inevitable part of life. She knows what it means to have been hurt. The woman is not in town yet, but is coming soon. She will stand out dramatically when you meet her. This will come to you; you do not need to pursue it."

Fine. That was for openers. From there, Sue went on to talk about other matters of interest—family and friends, work, health, money. And although she seemed to know many details intuitively, it dawned on me that her predictions didn't matter any more than my doubts. The real reason I was there was to open myself to the influence of her gentle clarity and vast faith in life's goodness. It made no difference whether we

hunted for the future in playing cards or shot tiddlywinks.
Some people open you to love by their very presence. As
Robert Bly wrote, if you want to write a poem about a pine
tree, go sit by a pine tree . . .

There's a wonderful joke about Abe, a devout Jew who
spent most of his life asking for little and getting less. One
day, he was alone in the shul, praying: "God, I know You're
busy, and I hate to take up Your time, but I need to ask You
something. All my life, I've been a poor man, and I'm not
getting any younger. I was thinking how nice it would be if
once, just once before I die, I could hit it big. God, do You
think, maybe, I could win the New York lottery?" A month
passed, nothing happened. So, Abe went back to the temple
and made an even more impassioned plea: "God, it's Abe
again. Remember? Last month I asked You if it might be
arranged I should win the New York lottery. Well, nothing's
happened, God, so I'm asking again. Please, God, just once,
let me win the New York lottery." Another month went by,
still nothing, and again, Abe returned to the synagogue. This
time, he prayed with all his heart: "God, it's me, Abe. I'm
sorry to bring this up again, but it's been already two months
and nothing's happened. Oh, God, please, please let me win
the lottery!" He had scarcely finished the thought when a
great rumbling ensued. The doors of the Holy Ark opened
and the voice of the Almighty Himself thundered forth: "Abe,
this is God. Meet Me halfway—*buy a ticket!*"

Now, there's a message in this joke that disturbs me even
while I'm laughing at it, the way Woody Allen's film *Zelig*
disturbed me—a spooky, furtive message creeping through
the humor. *Buy a ticket* . . . the phrase evokes a chorus of
associations in the psyche—of holding back and risking all,

of courage and fear, of decisive wins and irrecoverable losses—almost as though the tickets we buy and how we buy them measure our sanity, our humanness. Aristotle said that man is the knowing animal, but in view of how little we really know, it might be better to say that man is the animal that lives without knowing, the animal that buys tickets.

I remember when the lottery was introduced in Florida in 1988. Newspapers reported people standing in line at a local convenience store hours before it opened so they could get the first tickets issued. One front-page photo showed a man counting out bills to buy some five hundred tickets with what he later told reporters was his rent money. Maybe he saw what he was doing as an act of faith. I don't know. But this image strikes me as an apt metaphor for how those of us at the Grill had conducted ourselves in courtship. We pushed too hard, spent the rent money on a roll of the dice, gave away too much of ourselves too fast, all in the hope that some tremendous fulfillment would follow. And when the game was played out and we'd lost it all, we walked away heart-broken and disenchanted, vowing never to love anyone "that much" again. Maybe after losing the rent money for ten years or so, after losing his marriage and his kids and his job, the man in the convenience store turns out to be Abe. Alone, bereft, near the end of his life, he pleads with God to grant his lifelong wish, but he no longer has the courage or the strength to risk losing. Not again.

This idea of buying a ticket goes back a long way with me because of a short story I read when I was nine and never forgot. The story, written by Jack G. Finney and entitled "Of Missing Persons," goes something like this: A man whose life has become meaningless happens upon a small travel agency. Thinking that a change of surroundings might help, he goes inside and begins looking over several vacation brochures, none of which appeals to him. Then, he comes across one about a place called Verna that shows lush, rolling hills, softly rushing rivers, and beautiful, white-robed children and adults playing together in perfect contentment. The man inquires. "No," the travel agent says abruptly. "You don't want to go there. It's very expensive, and it's a one-way trip. You only get one ticket to Verna." "How much does it cost?" the man asks. "All you've got," answers the agent curtly. After persuading the travel agent to sell him the ticket, the man leaves and soon returns with his life savings—eight hundred dollars—in an envelope. The travel agent reluctantly accepts the money, then instructs the man to board a bus that will pick him up at a specified place around midnight.

As the appointed hour nears, our hero goes to where he's been told to wait for the bus. It's raining out, dark, miserable. The bus comes a few minutes late. The man boards and takes a seat, and the bus pulls away, eventually winding down remote and rain-flooded country roads. About a dozen other people sit on the bus in absolute silence. Finally, they arrive at an old barn. The driver instructs everyone to get out and go wait inside. The storm is growing worse. Between thunderclaps and lightning flashes, the passengers file out of the bus and into the barn, where they take seats on two hard benches and wait as told.

Sitting there with the others, our protagonist begins having serious second thoughts. Here he is, soaked to the skin, his shoes mud-covered, waiting in an abandoned barn somewhere with a bunch of strangers in the middle of the night. Eight hundred dollars, for this? It begins to dawn on him: He's been conned by a pro. Verna. Rolling hills. Paradise. Ten minutes pass. Fifteen. Finally, when he can't stand it any longer, he gets up and bolts for the door, cursing his stupidity. Once outside, he turns and slams the barn door shut in anger.

The force throws it back open just as a flash of lightning illuminates the inside of the barn. There, in the stark light, he sees the passengers walking toward the far wall, which has dissolved into a landscape of lush, rolling hills. Entering this idyllic world, they are welcomed by men, women, and children dressed in white robes. Another flash an instant later, and the barn is empty.

Stunned, the man begins walking along the dirt road and eventually makes his way home. The following day, he runs down to the agency to buy another ticket but the travel agent acts as though he doesn't know a thing about the transaction of the day before. He hands the man back the envelope with the eight hundred dollars in it, saying only, "You left this here yesterday."

In an epilogue of sorts, we learn that, after that, the man spent many years searching for obscure, hole-in-the-wall travel agencies in the hope of finding another ticket to the paradise he let slip from his hands, but all his efforts ended in vain. And every so often, he could hear the travel agent's voice echoing in his memory: "You only get one ticket to Verna . . ."

Nowadays, of course, there are an endless number of tickets to Verna, which is to say that there are none. Too many options confuse the mind and make for sloppy ticket buying. One young woman I knew, on the way to her wedding, said to me, "I figure we'll give it a try. If it doesn't work out, we can always get divorced." And I shuddered for her and her husband-to-be, whom I knew also, remembering the story of Verna and what happens in the crucial hour to those who go through the motions of giving "all they've got" but secretly hold back, who can't sit still with the tickets they've bought so that time can make its crucial contribution—like the farmer who planted seeds each morning, then dug them up each evening to see how they were doing. Within a year and a half, this young bride had fled from the barn of married life, back out into the storm of the world, feeling lonelier, more isolated, more confused, and less willing than ever even to go through the motions. Footnote: The man she left spent many anguished nights trying to figure out how *he* had failed *her*. The barn door we slam on our way out often catches somebody else's fingers.

I wonder why this woman did not give herself, why she bought her ticket so halfheartedly. I wonder why the man in the barn didn't sit there ten seconds longer than he did, or if by sitting there, filled with judgment and mistrust, he somehow kept the mysterious corridor to a better life from opening for the whole group. Mostly, I wonder if we're responsible for the tickets we buy, or if we're genuinely unable to do otherwise in a given moment, all things considered. Could the man in the barn have chosen to wait in faith? Could the bride have chosen to give herself fully and so, perhaps, receive fully? Over the years, our suffering, our losses, humble us, deepen us, soften us, and teach us to believe in more than our own willfulness—but do we have to lose our heart's desire to gain our faith? And until we've been humbled, deepened, softened, what do our so-called choices amount to but willful expressions of urges and limits that we do not determine but which, in fact, determine us? Aren't we as absurd as Abe in so much of our choosing—wanting and praying and waiting for a word that only we can speak, unaware of the part we might play in helping to create our own good? And at other times, aren't we like the fellow in the convenience store—overdoing, trading gentler balances and resolutions for drama and quick fixes? But when you reckon how much of our inner life is given to us, can we do otherwise? And if not, in what sense are we responsible for the "choice"—to do too little or do too much or hold back—that condemns us to further loss? Do any of us really make choices—little, transcendent creations ex nihilo? We may want to believe that we do, but aren't these so-called choices influenced, conditioned, shaped, even determined by the grip of the emotional baggage we carry, by our fears, the amount of courage available to us at a given time, the amount of information, the maturity, the clarity, the wisdom, the willingness or unwillingness to move forward—*none of these things themselves being chosen?* In light of all this, isn't there always only one choice: to acknowledge the contents of our own psyche and present ourselves, for better or worse, as we really are or to deny, hide, run away?

Brain-buzzing. It was this kind of root-canal thinking that once inspired a lover to say to me, "You're exhausting even with your clothes on." Trying to figure out this business about buying tickets *is* exhausting, an endless line of questioning that starts to sound like one of those fantastic Rube Goldberg inventions, rattling and spinning and sputtering without going anywhere or doing anything. Could it be that this kind of thinking is, itself, a way to avoid buying a ticket? When we've sustained enough direct hits in love, something shifts in the psyche. We become less willing to risk, less willing to buy a ticket. This isn't a conscious choice but a loss of heart, and it's a lonely place.

Courtship has to end before love can have a chance because courtship is about romantic projections and costumes while love is about getting naked with somebody else. It's easy to buy the courtship ticket, easy to give "all you've got" for that joyride. Love is another matter. That takes a lot of sitting still with ourselves, which is anything but easy. In this sense, the possibility of love is like the travel agency in Finney's story, and early involvement, which nowadays usually includes sex, is like buying a ticket from the travel agent

the way our hero did. We "fall" in love and eagerly make the
initial movement of buying a ticket, but at some point, the
bus comes along and we find ourselves going down dark
roads we didn't plan on. We may start to feel lost, like an
actor who's suddenly been thrown into the wrong movie.
And eventually, there we are in that damned barn, face to
face with our willingness or unwillingness to sit still through
those stormy times when we feel that there's no point to
things anymore, that we've been conned, that life is everywhere else, that we have to get up and run out into the night
or go mad. At that critical moment, we will make a choice.
And despite the furies that may be catapulting through the
ether of our psyche, despite our fear and ignorance and confusion and old patterns, we will be responsible for it, even if
by default, for we are the ones who will have to live with the
consequences.

Now, this may seem obvious, but the obvious is always
worth pointing out—it's so easily missed: Every ticket has its
price. Living alone isn't easy. Living with a partner isn't easy.
Only courtship is easy, and that's because courtship is a
dream from which two lovers eventually awaken when the
real differences between them assert themselves, when their
needs and wants conflict and their emotional patterns start
body-slamming each other to take control, when the charming, sublime, faultless darling to whom they were each irre-
sistibly drawn suddenly turns out to be a beer-slugging
Quasimodo or quirky hyena, and the "unattached" life starts
looking pretty good again. All of this suggests not only that
we should pick and choose carefully, but also that, since
every ticket has a price, we might want to get tough with the
brat in our psyche whose career seems to consist of trying to
get us to believe that we can have something without giving
something up.

This is the fatal error committed by the compulsive gambler in the convenience store, the bride, the man in the barn, and Abe. Their faith would move mountains but not furniture. They want, want, want—but nobody's willing to take care of business at home. They cha-cha through the world, buying tickets left and right, but they do not pay prices, they do not *give* themselves to the outcomes they say they want. If the man in the convenience store were willing to pay the price of his choices, he'd be using the rent money to pay the rent. The bride would be planning a marriage, not just a wedding— weddings are about marriage, after all, not about weddings. The man in the barn would be willing to be a fool to get to paradise—he had said he was willing to give everything, yet he held on to his reason and his cynicism and so denied himself passage. And Abe would buy a lottery ticket. In each case, there's a fundamental insincerity, a withholding of self, a focus on getting that misses the fundamentals.

This may be one reason that courtship is such a delicious time. However it happens, the lovers are absorbed in giving, and the joy they evoke in each other mirrors for them their own power to create goodness in a thousand little ways. How these bonbons turn into depth charges is beyond me, but they do, all too often. Still, I believe that we can discover in ourselves the capacity to create the same goodness in the sanity of love that we find in the divine madness of courtship.

Let me illustrate with yet another little story, this one personal, about a love relationship I have with somebody named "Jo." Actually, it's "JoJo," a beautiful, soft, petite, sulfur-crested cockatoo. Some years ago, and a million miles behind me in the emotional desert I crossed after my marriage ended, I found myself in a pet shop looking at parrots. I'd always loved birds and hadn't had one since I was nine or ten, about the same time I'd read Finney's short story. Even so, the birds of my youth had always been budgies, and now, although I knew that I was looking not only for a pet but for something I'd lost in my boyhood, I was ready for a *man's* bird, the kind that can take your arm off, goddam it—a peregrine falcon type that would dive out of the sky at my summons, a mighty *kree-ya, kree-ya* following her all the way down to my gauntleted arm, where she'd land, looking into my eyes with all the tamed fury of flight. Anyway, I got a cockatoo—a lovely creature, pure white with reddish eyes and a lemon-gold crest that opened like a dancer's fan, with various cockatooey flips of the head. All for just nine hundred bucks. (I must've wanted that piece of my boyhood pretty badly.)

Anyway, I took her home, set up a cage, and the courtship began. Within a few weeks, she settled down and let me handle her. Within a few months, we mastered responsive clucking and the old turn-the-bird-upside-down trick, among others, with a whole lot of hugging and kissing going on. We were in love. To my great delight, she wouldn't let other people anywhere near her. If they tried, they got hissed up one side and down the other and found themselves facing wings spread menacingly in the attack position; if they pushed it past that, the beak came into play. Jo was no falcon, but she was *my* bird, dangerous to anyone but me. It was wonderful.

After about six months, something happened. Jo started making, shall we say, a certain loud noise. Now, I don't mean hey-could-you-turn-down-that-radio loud, I mean spoon-down-the-garbage-disposal loud. I was sitting at the computer with my back to her the first time she did it, the first time this little ten-inch bird opened her throat and let out a train wreck. I thought I'd been shot. Somehow, the people at the pet shop failed to mention that cockatoos can make sounds unholy enough to send chills through a corpse.

The courtship was over. The second I walked anywhere near her, THE SOUND came at me like exploding glass, and if I scolded her, why, she just let it rip again. I started to hate the shrieking little bitch. The only way I found to stop her was to cover her cage. So Jo began living a reclusive life under the red Indian blanket; her talons grew needle-sharp, and I handled her less and less. She took to chewing her feathers and began to look ratty. Our love affair became a relationship of maintenance. I could feel nothing but contempt for her, and it seemed to me that we both deserved better. When I told my daughter, Samara, that I was "not enjoying the bird," she asked in her typical, intuitive way, "Are we talking divorce?" We were. The following week, I placed an ad in the local classifieds.

Two days later, a man from a nearby city called, asking about the bird, and we set up a time for him and his wife to come down and look her over. Charlie and Charlotte arrived the next evening. They told me that they had about fifty birds living in their aviary/garage, and it quickly became apparent that they had probably forgotten more about caring for our feathered friends than I'll ever know. They walked over to the cage, and Jo started doing her spitting-cobra imitation, but after about half an hour, she settled down.

Charlie and Charlotte love birds. They breed them and spend time with them and enjoy them. And for some reason, the conversation soon turned from the sale of Jo to the care of Jo. What was I doing? What was I not doing? Was I handling her a lot? Cockatoos, they explained, are like babies. They need a lot of attention. They need to feel a part of whatever's going on. Did I leave the radio or stereo on for her during the day when no one was home? Did I have any toys for her to play with? As they continued making suggestions, I opened the cage door, and Jo did something she had never done before, especially with strangers in the room. She hopped onto my hand, then ran up my arm and hid behind my neck, shivering slightly. She didn't know these people, but she knew me. In her way, she loved me. I was It for her, her one contact with another living creature, her safety zone, her human. I had "tamed" her, as Exupéry's Little Prince had tamed the fox, and now I was responsible for her. And my forgetting the love-bond between us, my neglecting her, my frustration with how badly our relationship had deteriorated, even my filing for divorce through the classifieds, had not changed the reality of that.

Charlie and Charlotte encouraged me to have Jo's nails and wings clipped, buy her some toys, increase her vitamin supplement, and start including her in the family. They told me to handle her more, talk to her—in short, to live up to the ticket I had bought. The next day, I took Jo to the local pet store where, much against her will, I had her wings and nails trimmed so that I could keep her on my hand for longer periods. I picked out a few toys I thought she'd like, bought some new, better seed mix for her, and got an open perch stand to set up in the living room so she could be nearer the action.

When I got her home and put her on her new perch, she was a bird transformed. It was startling. I put on some samba music, and she sat there for two hours, making little cooing noises and rocking gently to the music. And as I watched her, I started to feel love for her again, for this little creature that was dependent on me for its sense of place and well-being in the world. I had to face the fact that all of Jo's screeching had been an attempt to get my attention, to show me, in the only way she knew, how little I was giving. Only a day earlier, I was convinced that there was no recourse but to get rid of her, and that decision had seemed completely justified. But now, sitting in the living room, I could feel a new peace in the house, and a deep sadness came up from my stomach and heart into my throat as I suddenly thought of my divorce, and of how my marriage might have been saved if only my wife and I could have shifted our focus from what was wrong in each other to what we were doing to create what was wrong, and to what we might create instead. Looking at Jo perched sweetly there, I could *feel* the love again.

You may think that the moral to this story is a little bird-brained, but if we can't love our pets well, how will we ever love our partners well? The parallels are certainly there: It's easy to fall in love with a kitten or a puppy in a store, but taking care of it is hard, and our disenchantment can make us deaf to love's call not only to take care, but to give care. In so many ways, we, too, are birds in a cage crying out for love, and it isn't easy to give when our own neediness compels us to buy one ticket after another the way the man in the convenience store bought his lottery tickets, with no regard for what we're creating. Courtship can be a time when we search our heart for what it is that we truly want to give, what we want the life around us to be about—not just what we might get or win. Without this giving, we're in the same predicament as Abe, or the absent bride, or the man who never makes it to the Verna of his own wholehearted participation. Getting, winning—these are episodes of chance in which we hardly need participate. They happen *to* us, not *through* us. But courtship is about love, and love, whatever form it takes, is a call to care about ourselves and each other, not a lottery.

There's another joke about Abe—I don't know where these jokes come from. In this one, Abe's become so disheartened by life's losses and zits that he's finally embraced atheism. One day, his son stops him as he's preparing to go out the

door to meet his old friend Ira for Shabbat *services. "Papa,"
the son says, shaking his head, "you're such a hypocrite."
"Meaning what?" asks Abe, offended but willing to talk
about it. "Meaning," the son continues, "that you're an athe-
ist. Yet every Friday night without fail you go to synagogue
with Ira." "So, why a hypocrite?" asked Abe with innocence.
"Papa, you don't even believe in God!" insisted his son.
"Look," explained Abe, "Ira goes to shul to be with God. I
go to be with Ira." I really enjoy this joke, and like to believe
it describes Abe's life after the time of the lottery joke, since
this would mean that he learned how to buy a ticket.*

*I went to get a psychic reading to be with Sue. It was a
ticket well worth buying. Of course, the best and worst ticket
we buy is in allowing ourselves to love someone, because we
can never buy that ticket back. Love is forever. For better or
worse, we carry the people we've loved with us, either in the
unique fondness of who we were with them, or in denial. This
is a fact of psychic life—that love, like energy, is conserved
and transformed, never destroyed. Some feel threatened by
old ties and seek to put a muzzle on the psyche. Big mistake.
When the psyche is denied, it grows teeth and claws, and
comes chasing us in our dreams, perhaps eventually catching
us in the ambush of some bodily disorder or other, if necessary, to capture our shunted attention. So, there's far less to
fear in our continued caring for our earlier loves than in
slamming a door on the past and pretending that those loves
never happened. They happened; they were real. And they
live in us, still, as a source of richness or a source of symptoms. We owe it to ourselves to be careful about the tickets
we buy.*

Nothing Special

Yes, but the smell of enlightenment
is still too strong on you.
                    —Zen Roshi to a dying disciple

 *Every truth has its opposite truth.
That's a real bitch for the mind, which
incessantly demands a black-or-white
reduction of life's variegated colors.
And so, as it's true that we are wise to buy our tickets with
care, there is a corresponding truth that this ticket buying is
no big deal. Getting in step with life, with love, is more a side
order of broccoli than a hot fudge sundae. The daily diet
nourishes us; it doesn't shoot us into orbit. For those of us
who have shed hot tears in the middle of the night over the
end of a marriage that needed to end, who have torn the
pillowcase with our teeth and hated all creation because it
wouldn't manifest our self-destructive will, it takes some time
to acquire a taste for what's good for us. We tend to go after
flash, to pursue hotly, because our numbness has made it so
hard to feel anything at all that we're working with an ab-
normally high threshold. These emotional blast-offs tend to*

precede nosedives that end in splintering crashes, or, put less dramatically, they set us up for hurt and disappointment. So, over the years, the members of the Sunset Grill society began cultivating a new taste for life without drama. A taste for broccoli and the reliable ordinariness that makes such a good traveling companion along the way. And this has had a no-ticeable effect on how we are with the people we love. The places where we've stayed stuck and tended to recreate the pain of the past are precisely the places where we still con-sider ourselves, our desires, our will, our love, to be just a little special . . .

One night at an Al-Anon meeting, I was going on and on about my parents or my right to express myself or something, when an unassuming and exceptionally bright guy named Art asked me why I thought my pain was so important, and for the life of me I didn't know. There was a long moment of attentive silence in the group while my mind fumbled for an answer, a justification. Then, I started laughing as it dawned on me that the emotional pain I had been stuck in most of my life really was no big deal, nothing special. We all have some of it, often much more than we let on. Somehow, in this recollection of the whole, the pain of the past dissipated. The only thing left was the laugh.

At some point, all of this business about "my pain" and "my family dysfunction" and "my codependent pattern" can come into a wonderful perspective that throws open the prison door called "specialness" and shows us that we're all part of something greater that includes each other. Instead of continuing to loiter in the mind's alleys of martyrdom, self-pity, blame, and an inflated sense of self, we get to walk out into the neighborhood, take a deep breath of rustling trees and blue sky, and see what's there, see the miraculous ordi-

nariness of being alive. And in this, we get to belong
again—to ourselves, to the world as it is, to the living present.
Once we can really let the truth of our ordinariness touch us
emotionally, something deep refocuses. In place of all that
brain-babble and endless running around the world chasing
It, suddenly, we have the moment, we have here and now.
Complaining becomes ludicrous and the martyr within us,
whom nobody ever liked, finds himself out of a job. We no
longer *feel* that life is unfair or that we are its special victims.
Rather, we *see* that we're all in this thing together, doing the
best we can.

The ancient Chinese Zen principle of *wu shih* sums up the
secret to sane living in two words: *nothing special*. The term
also implies "natural," "unaffected," and "in a state of effortless harmony." When clouds drift through the sky, it is
wu shih. The look in an infant's eye—that, too, is *wu shih*.
Now, the mind regards itself and its thoughts as special, so
it's never satisfied with the ordinary and drives us relentlessly
with the nagging notion that something or other out there
will make us happy and whole, which, of course it never does
for long. Making things special—the promotion, the involvement with this or that person, the salary increase, having a
baby—is the deeply rooted habit that keeps us out of the
sufficiency of simply being who we are, right now, in the
moment at hand. By the same token, when we make our love
relationships into something special, we've already wandered
off the path and into the woods. Loving well, like living well,
is nothing special. It's about coming back to earth, to what's
most common, most natural, to what's right under our nose
and our feet.

So, we need to remember, especially in love, that we're
losing our sense of having to be special and our grandiosity
and our martyrdom and coming home to the simplicity of the

ordinary, to things as they are, to *wu shih,* to "nothing special." This is really all there is to growing up, since, to be simply who we are is to be willing to step outside the child's narcissistic fantasy world and take part in *this* world, the real world. We can, of course, step back into that fantasy world as we may wish—it is, after all, a wonderful and boundless source of energy and creativity—but that's not the same as living there, as failing to see that it *is* a fantasy world, an overlay. Entering the real world, the world of "nothing special," means above all, accepting our impermanence, accepting things as they are rather than demanding that they be the way we want them to be. This is an important step along the zigzagging road to love. It means entering fully into our small role, into the details of each moment as it is without the compulsion to diminish or exaggerate it. As one Zen patriarch put it, the enlightened man sees the passing of his life like the falling of a leaf—not because a life is such a trivial thing, but because the falling of a leaf is so simply and fully what it is.

Getting over the feeling of being privileged in pain can seem damned near impossible. It's like the woman who realizes she's been living her life under the shadow of a "look what a good girl I am" complex, so she makes an inner move to shake that off and the very next thing she's doing is wondering if she's a good girl for having shaken it off. The delusion of specialness has a way of reconstituting itself like this even while we're dismantling it with our best awareness, the way water opens up around rocks and then resumes its course undisturbed. So, waking up from the drama of specialness takes time.

These understandings become useful only when they're put into practice, because if we begin with theory, it's easy to stay with theory and lose the real benefit. If we begin with just some *idea* that we're not special, no different from anybody else, we may secretly believe that our realizing this makes us just a little different, just a little special, and there we are again, or still, with the right idea but nothing to show for it. Instead, we can begin with the practical. Since, whether we believe it or not, we *aren't* special, we can, in each moment that the feeling of specialness arises, simply dismiss it as the eternal nonsense of the mind. For example, I may feel depressed, or lonely, or confused on a certain day. No big deal. But my mind can seize this mood and start spinning self-escalating spirals of analysis, projection, doom thinking, blame, neediness—you know. So, as soon as I recognize that this is happening, I can make a decision to ignore it because I know that all of this mind-stuff is about the drama of being special, which I already know I'm not. My mind, eternal salesman that it is, can rattle on—it always has and always will, but I don't have to buy what it's selling. Another example: Let's say that a book I write is published and people are congratulating me. Now, I notice that I'm not feeling much about it, that I'm in a kind of denial, and I become aware that this numbness is flowing from an old belief that I'm too special to enjoy a success—a hangover from the martyr role. At that point, I can choose to start responding to the excitement and words of appreciation, to start acknowledging them, not because there's anything special about the book coming out but precisely because there isn't. Choosing to enjoy it doesn't mean that I can necessarily choose to *feel* the enjoyment, but practice shows that the feeling never trails too far behind the decision.

There's a famous Zen saying: "The Way is not difficult for him who has no preferences." This, of course, doesn't mean that we'll be better off if we prefer to not have any preferences; rather, it suggests that living fully involves a spirit of cooperation with natural forces. *Wu shih.* Dennis puts it this way: If you're carrying a large piece of plywood in a stiff wind, you have two options. You can carry it face into the wind, like a sail, in which case you're in for a hell of a fight. Or, you can, with the slightest adjustment, turn the thing sideways so you're carrying it edge-first. As soon as you do, of course, the resistance is gone. You're still there. The board is still there. So is the wind. What's gone is the struggle.

Imagine what would happen if we rediscovered the charm of fully participating in the life we already have: our car with the missing window crank, our home with the botched kitchen wallpaper, our husband or wife who leaves the dresser drawers open. There's great entertainment in all of this if we can just get through to it. You see, we might find ourselves so tickled with being right where we are that we wouldn't feel the compulsion either to "make it wrong" or to rush out and "make it right" in some fantasy. Instead, we might go shopping for a window crank, or some new wallpaper, or start leaving funny little love notes in every open drawer. We might actually begin *receiving* life rather than racing around trying to take it by storm in all those wrongs and rights that leave us with no peace and, in the end, only give us more to undo. To find this joy, to open our awareness to the giggle of simply being here, now, we have to stop running and be still long enough for the moment to reach through the cluttered awareness we habitually bring to it. We have to stop fighting the wind.

It helps to explore these things firsthand, to experiment with them, and find out for ourselves. There *is* a great joy in simply being where we are, in seeing through the illusion of specialness and all our attempts to "improve" life. Of course, none of this means that we won't have problems. It means that when problems arise, we'll be practiced in being present with them, and it's always in being present that solutions to problems become apparent. If we're sad, or lonely, or in pain, being present certainly doesn't mean that we won't feel these things. On the contrary, we'll feel them fully, and we'll feel the *comfort* of feeling them fully. It takes consistent practice to cultivate and strengthen this awareness of the sufficiency of the moment, so it's a good idea to begin. We can sit with the truth of whatever we're feeling, with as much stillness and as little resistance as possible. We can develop that much openness, attentiveness, and honesty. And in practicing these, we're teaching ourselves how to be in love.

When my marriage ended, it was as though I forgot how to be. There was no present—only the hope of reunion and a deluge of memories, both poignant and painful, that didn't let up for years. Eventually, though, I stopped fighting and accepted that things weren't going to go the way I wanted. Then I started to sit with the truth of that. At first, it was like sitting in the front row of a movie theater and watching nonstop horror films. But gradually, this, too, subsided, and I was able to discern, slightly, the inscrutable "suchness" of the moment, as the Buddhists call it. This is difficult to describe, but it felt as if someone had opened a skylight in a dark cave. I was alive, you see, and in the breaking of my heart, my illusions about my will had also been broken. There was room in my awareness for the simple, ordinary miracle of my being alive to present itself, apart from the pain and the longing and the drama that had tyrannized too many days to count. And in that revelation of the ordinary was a trace of everything I'd ever wanted in a partner or a job or anything else.

From this, I learned that it's all a grab bag, and that it is our losses, not our victories, that make us more than we were. Sometimes I still feel lonely. But not as lonely as I was then, when I was without myself, without the stillness, without the living moment, sleepwalking in a private dream of willfulness I called life. Now, I can look at the cat stretching on the hardwood floors, or listen to the afternoon storm clouds rumbling in the distance, or watch my fingers as they type words that I do not first have to think, and it's enough. And in every ordinary, unspecial detail is the joy, the rush, the belly laugh of somehow being alive and part of it all.

Speaking of details, here's a great Zen parable: This monk is being chased by a ferocious and hungry tiger. Just as the monk feels that his strength is about to give out, the tiger chases him right over the edge of a cliff where, at the last second, the monk grabs on to a vine and stops his fall. Looking down, he sees another tiger on the ledge below. Just then, a mouse comes out of a hole and starts gnawing through the vine. Suddenly, the monk notices a ripe, red strawberry growing on the vine, and (this is the best part) he picks the strawberry and eats it. Delicious!

Now, maybe I'm wrong, but the moral of this story sounds awfully familiar. Isn't this also what *The Wizard of Oz,* that indelible film from our collective childhood, had to say? Dorothy longs to be somewhere else, somewhere "over the rainbow," and soon finds herself there. She goes on all kinds of special adventures with special characters, each seemingly lacking an essential personality trait that Dorothy herself has. But her greatest ally, ironically, is her homesickness. Practically from the time she arrives in this extraordinary world, her purpose becomes simply to get back to Kansas—plain old, flat, ordinary, nothing-special Kansas—and she remains true to this purpose despite the glitter of Munchkin Land and promises of honor, despite all the magic tricks and captivating scenery, despite fear and, ultimately, even the threat of death. In the end, each of Dorothy's friends learns that he has always possessed the quality he came to Oz to find. And Dorothy learns that this world of yellow-brick roads, witches, and wizards is really no more than a magician's trick, a mirror, a razzle-dazzle song and dance that has left her heart empty and aching for the people and places she loves most. Only when all else has failed—that's crucial to the story—does the Good Witch appear to tell her that what she needs to save her, what she needs to get back home, has been with her from the beginning. All she has to do is click her heels together three times and say, "There's no place like home." As soon as she does this, she wakes up from the dream that she was far away to find that she's been home all along.

Can it be that simple? That, no matter what, home is always right under our feet and as close as our remembering? Like Dorothy, like the monk who eats the strawberry, we can come home to the present moment and learn to savor its sweetness. Just under the thin facade of all our busyness, the joy of being alive is here, now, waiting for us to wake up, on *this* side of the rainbow, in our own backyard.

There's nothing special in the way the earth smells after it rains, or in the slow, rippling mime of birds flying in formation, but something about these things calls forth love in us and reminds us that we're part of the great, wonderful whatever moving everywhere. If we can open ourselves to such simple moments, when the world is at its most innocent, maybe we'll be able to open ourselves to love with a partner. As this ordinary, undramatic vision takes hold in us, we see its calming, steadying influence in every area of our lives. And as we continue to open ourselves to it, we feel a renewed sense of optimism about love, whose ordinariness is the most exquisite ordinariness of all, like the hushed roundness of a pearl.

PARTNERSHIP

But one man loved the pilgrim soul in
   you
and loved the sorrows of your changing
   face . . .

—W. B. Yeats
"When You Are Old"

Coming Together

We went every place together.
We did everything.
We fell in love.
I fell in love,
She just stood there.

—Woody Allen
Bananas

 *Dennis will be only too glad to tell you about our first attempt at "picking up girls." We were sixteen in those tossed-salad days, and had just got our driver's permits. A 1963 Dodge Dart and the weekend unleashed us to make the traditional macho-run along Collins Avenue on Miami Beach, where there was never a dearth of beautiful women, especially for three teenagers with endocrine systems secreting high-octane testosterone round the clock. I say "three" teenagers because George was with us then, our crazy Greek-Italian buddy who liked to march around the house in his underwear pretending to play the trumpet while Herb Alpert and the Tijuana Brass ripped through his house and several others in the neighborhood. On this particularly ill-fated Friday night, George was unavailable, so Dennis and I were forced to enter into battle without him. As we parked*

the car and got out, the sea air smelled daring and full of promise. We began walking south on the ocean side of Collins; the hotels weren't as densely placed then, and you actually could see stretches of beach in between. In a little while, we spied two attractive young women walking about thirty paces ahead. They were dressed to kill, a strategy that was working extremely well, especially on Dennis and me. A few minutes later, they crossed Collins and started walking back the other way, obviously cruising. Dennis and I quickly assessed the situation, then crossed the street and resumed shadowing the young women. Suddenly, I was struck by an inspiration: Why not quicken our pace and actually pass *them? I'm not sure what I had in mind here. Maybe I thought that if we got ahead of them, they would then be good enough to start following* us, *relieving us of the responsibility to engage, which I was fast doubting I really wanted anyway. But my loins had no doubt, and for the time being, they were in charge. So, Dennis and I closed the gap between us and our would-be companions, moving deftly around them the way the tracks of a cartoon skier move impossibly around a tree, regrouping on the other side. Now, during the few seconds that we were a foursome all in a row, I was sure that I overheard distinct strains of Spanish. "Hey," I whispered to Dennis, "they're Spanish. Let's make our move." The logic of this, too, escapes me now, but I guess I felt that having done just that little bit of recon would somehow bring the whole thing off. "Okay," I said to Dennis, like a bad ventriloquist. With that, we wheeled around and confronted our two señoritas. "Buenos noches," I said suavely, blowing all my Spanish in one breathless salvo. "Would yoo care four ay drrrr-ink?" I asked, trilling like a canary. To this phonetic embarrassment, the shorter of the two women, a yummy brunette in a ruffly red dress, said in perfect English,*

"Where?" Okay, time out. At sixteen, you can handle "No."
Nothing to it—you get so much practice. You may even be
able to handle "Yes," though it's doubtful. But "Where?"
This was a trick answer, definitely not on the program. Never
at a loss for a wrong move, I put my fingertips together so
that my hands and arms formed the apex of a roofline, and
asked, "Howard Johnson's?" At least my voice didn't crack.
I don't think. Anyway, the damage was done. Our lovelies
looked at each other and smiled forbearingly at the sweet
monkeys we had suddenly become. Then, with no Spanish
accent whatsoever, the ruffly red dress said, "Maybe some
other time." They went on their way, and that was the end of
that. Except that Dennis has never let me forget it.

I've been trying for three weeks to write this chapter on
sex, and now I'm trying again. Each time, after waxing poetic
for ten pages or so, I'd remember that I didn't know what the
hell I was talking about. In one draft, for example, I thought
I should pursue the idea that sex isn't merely physical
release—that turning sex into a consumer good is just one
more way we snack on the sacrament, and bad us. But the
more I pursued, the faster the idea ran away, like one or two
lovers I've known. I could make a start, write pages, go
through the motions, but somehow, we weren't really coming
together. So, I let that one go.

Then I went off on a thing about AIDS and Eros. Damned
impressive, a left-brain tour de force. Night after night, I
sculpted the piece, adding shape here, texture there. Then, for
no reason I could explain, I started feeling apprehensive. I
chewed my fingernails until they were tattered, and began to
spend a lot of time fantasizing torrid bedroom scenes.

That's how I leave my body—by biting my fingers and

biting imaginary women on the neck, among other places. Now, when this sort of activity takes hold, invariably there's something that I don't want to feel. Which is why, when I finally do manage to catch myself deep in thought, I let my awareness settle back into my heart, stomach, and gut— check out the weather down south. This time, what I found there was fear. And I realized that the fear was being stirred up by my trying so hard to make sense of this tremendously complex subject, by my feeling that I *have* to make sense of it (what would a book about love and relationships be without a chapter on sex, after all?) and by my knowing in my heart of hearts and gut of guts that I *can't* make sense of sex because sex doesn't make sense to me.

So, at two in the morning, when sleep is just another wide-awake thought, I ask myself: What am I afraid of? And from the corner of the room, something that feels like me whispers: *Coming together.* The reference is clearly sexual, and as I lie there, wondering, scanning the darkness for some direction, suddenly the stillness opens, and out flood images of lying on the living room floor like nested spoons with the woman I love, of peeling off perfumed clothes, a glass of water on the night table ... then arguments, a separation followed by endless hours of clock-watching in disbelief, racing home during lunch hours to check the mail, angry outbursts and dismal appeals that came to nothing. These phantoms take shape and crawl into bed with me, driving some invisible wedge deeper, and I forget for a moment who I am. As the darkness fills up with memory, suddenly there's a chill, a marrow-sense that maybe all that loss, all that pain was nothing personal— that after the dust of dreams and marital promise had settled, what was left was one pattern of ancient hurt doing battle with another. And somehow, *despite the love*—an awful phrase—despite the love and all that was good, it was these patterns that had the relationship in the end. Or are these just the ramblings of the sleepless and disconsolate, long after a fact that knew no real rhyme or reason, but simply was what it was?

Nearly three o'clock now, and the voice in the corner has grown more insistent: *Coming together!* Yes—all right, but what is it that's supposed to come together? The images continue to flow: I remember a white satin robe, playfully using the sash to give unexpected pleasure—the sudden, wide eyes and willing smile, the tiny sounds. And I remember an orgasm that *was* an orgasm—the love bursting open and out of me like a soundless geyser. I was so startled when that happened the first time, when holding her under me—we were all hands and mouth and warmth—I came with all my heart and the word *wife* brushed my lips like a kiss from God. Suddenly, lovemaking was more "love" than "making." Something took over, something far more inner and more compelling than biological programming, and it swept me up and along like a leaf in a hurricane. Sorrow, joy, adoration, trust, gratitude, grief, nonsense, even anger and possessiveness—all of these surfaced in a single moment of fullness and exhaustion that left me shaking like one of those vibrating beds in a southern motel. Three-thirty. Still no chance of sleep. Only the feeling that there is something I have to find in this weary urgency, some sense to make of love and loss.

Coming together. Do I really know anything about sex, anything at all? Well, I know that you have to take off your clothes to do it. Now there's probably some guy in the Guinness book who's done it in deep-sea diving gear. But that doesn't matter. To make contact, you first have to expose what's usually hidden underneath. Again: *What we want to touch is what's usually hidden underneath,* and this is just as true of psyches as it is of bodies. Hidden underneath our calm, cool, socialized exterior, our plans and strategies and conscious will, is the truth of who we are, what we feel, what we are carrying in denial. Sometimes this truth erupts into our awareness, at which point we can acknowledge it and let it in, come together with it, or resist it and push it back down into the anonymous catacombs of the spirit. In our relation to this truth, we're *all* feminine: We can't put ourselves *into* this truth; we can only open ourselves to it, receive it, let it rise inside us and fill us with its healing presence.

This coming together with what is true in us can be scary because it means coming into receptive relation to something greater, something that we can't control. You know, the truth within us might tell us that we have to leave a loveless marriage, or stay in a difficult one, or stop running from the past and start cleaning it up. It might tell us that we've been lying, that we're selfish, hypocritical, grandiose. It might call us to be more than we've settled for and plunge us into the sheer depth of our most secret feelings and possibilities. This truth, which waits patiently, whispering to us from the dark room of the psyche, speaks to us of what we've always known but were unwilling to admit. To surrender to this truth *as our own*, to own up to it and own it, means to stop denying, apologizing, explaining, and most of all, to stop projecting it onto the world and running around in circles chasing it. Letting our emotional truth into our consciousness and taking responsibility for it as ours is frightening because we may find ourselves carried to the brink of a new necessity, to an awareness that there's something that must be done, and so it is often the harbinger of decisive change. This is even true of sexual coming, which begins with movement that is more or less volitional but defers increasingly to something greater until it isn't a matter of choice anymore. A synapse is jumped, a threshold crossed, and we're "taken over" by something else, something overwhelming, undeniable, final—a "little death," as the French call it.

Sometimes it seems that there's no end to the rites of passage we have to go through. So, when a man, through grace or gumption or both, finally *does* come with all his heart, he is almost certain to make the mistake of believing that this nearly overwhelming sensation of love and union is about his beloved, who, in fact, at that same sublime moment may be thinking about tomorrow's sale at Bloomingdale's or whatever. Transported by the physical and emotional overflowing, he may easily miss the fact that this profound wave of passion, adoration, oneness, is arising *within him,* that it's *his* psyche, not his beloved's, that has penetrated his ordinary consciousness and given him this profound sense of union. Regardless of her intentions, her inner gifts, or her awareness of what is happening to him, he may come away believing that she is the source of the experience. And as long as he mistakes his psyche for an outer condition in this way, as long as he doesn't wake up to this projection and recognize the true source within himself, the two of them are in for a bad time of it. He will keep expecting her to live up to a stature reserved for the gods and goddesses who dwell within each of us. She, of course, will never be able to carry that off, and the ordinariness that sooner or later characterizes all healthy intimacy will seem to him to be the most heartbreaking disappointment rather than a path leading to greater clarity, sharing, and individuation. And if the lover who has been so unfortunately saddled with this burden of living up to another's inwardness should leave the relationship, the one left will experience the loss of his partner as the loss of his very self. The way to prevent this mess is for each partner to live up to the richness of his or her own inner life and take responsibility for his or her projections as soon as possible.

Taking responsibility for our projections involves participating in these intensities as inner events, and not making our partner responsible for providing us with such grand feeling. To each other, what more can we ever be, at best, than fallible? There is so much wonderful ordinariness that must fill the long gaps between those remarkable moments of ecstasy. None of us can stay in the rarified atmosphere of Olympus for long. To make gods and goddesses, or for that matter, daughters or fathers, sons or mothers, out of our partners is to project our own capacity for inner approach and union, and so to evict ourselves from our own body. No good can come of it. In a year or two, when the inner images no longer stick as well to the person onto whom we've stuck them, there is bound to be a great sense of disappointment, even betrayal—and all due to a colossal case of mistaken identity.

Perhaps we can't draw a hard line: Our passion is about our partner, too, after all; if it were strictly an inner event, we'd have a heck of a time figuring out why some people seem to inspire and evoke these highs while others leave us flat. But this will be little consolation if we're living within the smothering embrace of a projection, and the preciousness of our partner doesn't absolve us of responsibility for our own inner truth. Lies kill relationships, and a projection is a consummate lie that keeps two people separated by fostering the illusion that the one is the other. Coming together emotionally with another depends on our willingness to become more and more who we are, and at the same time, to be more and more transparent, more and more honest in the other's presence. For this to happen, each partner must defer to the *authority* of his or her prolific psyche, and so move beyond mood-driven willfulness. Only this inner acquiescence can keep the fires of love, celebration, gratitude, intimacy, and deepening commitment alive in the face of the inevitable discrepancies, setbacks, and frustrations of the outer life. A deeper love becomes possible when we take responsibility for our own ecstasy.

This responsibility isn't limited to the bedroom, nor to our loftier sentiments. It encompasses our demons as well as our angels. Take anger, for example. There's nothing wrong with my feeling angry because you're twenty minutes late. That anger is mine; it is not only my right but my responsibility to acknowledge, express, and release it. But if I express it by trying to make you responsible for it, I'm not doing a very good job of loving either of us. The projected consciousness has a hard time understanding that it's possible to express anger without blame, to own it without swallowing it. I can slobber and growl and say, "I'm so angry!" without dumping that anger on you, as in: "You're late! You never give a damn about keeping me waiting!" and so on. If I'm feeling sick to my stomach, I may need to vomit; that doesn't entitle me to vomit all over you. The same is true with being sick at heart. And if I can remember to stay that responsive to my truth, that responsible, if I can keep from placing you in the cross hairs of *my* mood, even though you may have wittingly or unwittingly played a part in the circumstances that brought it on, maybe you'll find that there's room for you to come closer to me and even help me to honor the angry spirit within me rather than jumping into the role of martyr or persecutor. You might offer something like, "I know you're angry. It is frustrating to be kept waiting like that." Interestingly, "I'm sorry" isn't even needed. And if you want to come together even more with your power to be and to be responsible, you might add, "What can I do to make it up to you? What can I do that would please you?" That's great foreplay, a rich mix of strength and tenderness. Now, if you try that approach and you're dealing with a projection, you might get back something punishing like, "Yeah, you can make damned sure you're never late again!" which is dirty fighting because for a lover, the point isn't to blame or punish but to honor and work with his emotional reality. Clean fighting retains self-intimacy and self-responsibility, which means it has all the intensity and passion of fighting without an enemy. And while your partner is struggling, in the heat of the moment, to own his anger, any offering you can make that respects his effort will have a tremendous healing effect. This sort of gesture can appease an angry spirit very quickly—it wants to be acknowledged, you see—but for the most part, we don't treat each other like that. We're too lost outside ourselves. So we throw our weight around, point fingers, snap daggers at each other we wish we could take back later, and generally make each other and ourselves miserable. And we end up apart even though our heads may be sleeping on the same pillow.

I've been rambling, and I don't know where it's taken me. The luminous dial beside me reads 5:26, and sleep is finally near. The darkness in the room has softened some. No voices remain, no fantasies. I smile. Over the past five years, my psyche has sent its roots deep down into me. I can feel them now, and I'm grateful. The clock is ticking more softly, as though not to disturb. Outside, the slate gray clouds of night tumble silently by the window, and I take a deep breath that leaves me as a sigh. I close my eyes. At the border of sleep, one last image comes: the ancient Ouroborus—the snake that forms a circle by biting a piece of tail it doesn't seem to know is its own. As my consciousness eases into the other world, the Ouroborus speaks to me, and I recognize its voice as the one that whispered earlier from the corner of the room. *Coming together.* In touching what is hidden, I have come back to myself, to where I started. And in the morning, on my way to the Sunset Grill for breakfast, it will occur to me that this is how we always recognize our own truth—by what we keep coming back to. Looking out through the Grill's soaring atrium windows, I'll watch the morning storm clouds grow dark and heavy and finally let go, according to their nature. And right there, in front of God and everybody, with rain running down the glass like tears, I'll have an orgasm without even coming.

I've quit trying to pick up women. That game wore out when I finally stopped projecting long enough to realize that this sort of sex and romance had little to do with sex and romance and a great deal to do with wanting to feel like a man: If she smiles, I'm a man. If she applauds, I'm a man. If she's pleased, I'm a man. If she goes to bed with me, I'm really a man. But if she does none of the above, here comes the urgency, the withdrawal, the anxiety, the itchy craving for the sweet painkiller of romantic distraction, the female fix. And since the pain that all this fixing is supposed to fix isn't about a woman to begin with, but about the need to heal a deeply compromised masculine identity, the whole routine is hopeless—like looking under a street lamp for a quarter you lost three blocks down the road because the light is better. Masculine identity and confidence can't be cultivated by pleasing or performing or cutting notches in a box of condoms, but only by reclaiming our projections and participating wholeheartedly in the details of life. There's an alchemy in this participation that transforms work into worship, adds ritual to the routine, and turns everyday responsibilities into acts of love, service, and self-expression. Being right and being tough are not manly. Neither is fighting wars. Sports can be manly because they hold up an ideal of physical excel-

lence. But winning at all costs isn't manly, because it lacks spirit, and manliness, like womanliness, is spiritual, a psychic value. Leaving things at least a bit better than you found them is manly. Refusing to be a victim is manly. Coming together is manly. So is going shopping.

Real Men Go Shopping

As we live, we are transmitters of life . . .
even if it's only in the whiteness
of a washed pocket-handkerchief.
                                    —D. H. Lawrence
                                    "We Are Transmitters"

 *The various Twelve-Step programs, all of which take their cue from Alcoholics Anonymous, are known for their slogans and terse phrases, such as "tough love." Some people think that this term is a contradiction; I think it's redundant. For me, love has always been tough. Once the cooing of courtship has settled down, there are the daily details, the thousand angels and demons that closeness to another human being invariably brings up.*

One thing that's made partner-love especially tough for me is the fact that, like many men, I have a hard time feeling things when they happen. For example, on many occasions, without even realizing it, I've thrown honest anger to the lions in order to appear kind and understanding. But beneath the nice-guy act, without even realizing it, I was keeping score and carrying a grudge. This "kindness" proved to be a lousy deal for all concerned because eventually the anger,

triggered by some silly blooper or other, spewed out as rage. Instead of getting mad over, say, someone's taking advantage of me, I'd offer a benevolent smile and a "that's okay," then two days later, shriek at the cat for getting Tender Vittles on the floor.

Now, it wasn't just anger that I felt I had to fire off sideways like this; grief also had to be subverted. When I learned that a friend of mine got himself killed in a car accident, I felt shock, two seconds of outrage, and then, nothing, just as I had when family members had died during my life. Always, this nothing, this emotional digging in and breath-holding— then, later, a trivial incident or stray memory would set off the time bomb, and the inner fortification against feeling would collapse without warning, exposing me to a flood of sorrow that belonged to decades earlier and contained a current of despair that seemed, somehow, added.

Believe me, this ability to go numb and then overreact later puts something of an edge on the everyday dealings of love because it is self-camouflaging and can mask what's really going on. Often, just at the moment of greatest closeness between two people, all hell breaks loose over nothing, and if you can peek past the ego-defenses, the knee-jerk reactions, the sheer momentum of the thing, you discover that nobody really knows why it's happening. Until the lovers get clear on what's running them aground, there's little hope of either finishing whatever's being emotionally blockaded or assessing the triggering situation properly, in the context at hand and so, working things out together. Anger doesn't have to be rage; grief doesn't have to be depression. The cat isn't making demands on me when she gets Tender Vittles on the kitchen floor. She's not taking advantage. She's not conspiring to make my life difficult. She's eating. She's being a cat. And most of the time she's a far sight better at that than I am at *being a human, even though I almost never get food on the floor.*

Emotional resistance spoils things when the details of the present become corrupted by the bleedthrough of habitually forestalled feeling. They keep us from being, and so, certainly, from being in love. To live well, to love well—both depend on a willingness to enter into the moment as it is, to give and take without the censorship of past and future agendas, to discover something new in the familiar. Now, "living in the living present" sounds good, but what does it mean? It means paying attention, listening not only with our ears, but with our heart. It means telling the truth, giving that to the unfolding of things. None of this is grand philosophy. It's simple. Most of all, living in the living present means taking the details seriously, as though they contain all that matters. They do.

It isn't necessarily true that the sins of the parents are visited upon the children. I found this out by going shopping. Now, this phrase "going shopping" usually sends a chill through a man's spine. Real men aren't supposed to go shopping; in fact, they're supposed to hate it. This was certainly the example set for me by my father, who preferred to wait out in the car with his old friend, the radio, and listen to a ball game. Or drop my mother off and come back for her. The few times there was no game, or a return trip was too inconvenient, or she needed him to carry something, he reluctantly went along, suffering every evil minute of it. I can still see him checking his watch, stewing nervously while my mother floats from one sale rack to another. Within a matter of minutes, his jaw begins to tighten, then the looks start, and in the end, there's the restrained race back out to the parking lot with Dad well in the lead.

Let me be more specific about what I mean by *shopping*. I don't mean going to the store to buy electronics. That's a man's purchase. So are hardware, building or repair materials, tools, and anything that has to do with how the car runs. These *hard* things stock the consumer shelves of manhood, and a man never says, thinks, or feels that he's going "shopping" when he goes to the store to buy any of them. The purchase of hard goods is a matter of necessity, while the very word *shopping* has something soft about it—curiosity, the let's-see-what-we-can-find spirit of a field trip, an absence of conclusions. A woman has no idea of what she may buy when she goes shopping. She goes to find out. A man, on the other hand, never goes shopping, even when he heads to the store to buy something. This is why women tell their friends simply that they're "going shopping," while men say that they have to go "pick up" the new television or a new woman or whatever. "Picking up" is physical labor. It's manly. He just hoists his belt, spits into his hands, and "picks it up."

The model of manliness I inherited is the one most baby-boomers got from fathers who had been flayed by the Depression and the War. These were the unforgiving hands that shaped their character, that grabbed them by the scruff of the neck and hung them on the meat hook of survival. And this is what their lives were about. Financial mistakes could mean ruin. Failing to follow through could kill you. So, as a cultural imperative produced by the times, you worked long, hard hours, sometimes over a hundred a week—and if you didn't do as you had to, as you were *told* to by economic necessity, if you reflected on the meaning of your life a little too much, your family didn't eat. Later, many of these men, upon retiring from a lifetime of labor, would feel as though they *were* dying, and more than a few actually did, having lost all sense of place and purpose. The yoke of work became their life-support system, and while their children, freed up by the relativities of the new science and the sixties, would argue with them that life is more than work, and that their retirement gave them the chance they'd never had or taken to get to know themselves, to be themselves, to do what *they* wanted to do, the old saying applied with a vengeance: "Says easy, does hard." Besides, what they *wanted* to do was what they had always done, which was work.

Dostoevski wrote novels about the "peasant dignity" of this kind of man, for whom life *is* struggle, who is in a way, always at war, destroying bridges so that he can rebuild them. What Dostoevski didn't tell us, modern life has made all too clear: This man is incapable of getting away from it all because he always takes it with him. And how does he relax? By watching competitive sports, another battlefield complete with goals, gains, and losses. Going shopping is, for him, unsettling in the extreme—a little death that swings its scythe each god-awful minute he's standing around looking at this or that with no real sense of mission accomplished or plan fulfilled, no structure. Such a man was more prepared to deal with the anxiety of combat than the anxiety of browsing in a mall for a few hours.

There are, of course, exceptions. I know because I'm one of them. I love to go shopping. Not only as women do, but *with* a woman. For *soft* goods. And not with me leading the way, but more tagging along, which is to say that I love to do what other men detest: to "stand around" while she browses, checks out the sale racks, and—this is the best part—tries on a dozen outfits, coming out of the dressing room after each one to get my opinion. It would drive my father out of his skull.

There was never any concession in this for me, because I discovered that going shopping can be a terrific way to fall in love again with the woman you love. All the ingredients are there—excitement, for example. With the man along, the woman isn't just trying things on. She's *presenting* them, and herself along with them. To a man. *Her* man. Suddenly, she has the most important guy in her life as a potential admirer, someone to please besides herself, and this stokes the fire nicely. Along with excitement, there's an element of newness, even shyness. She comes out of the dressing room wearing crimson culottes, and you can see the self-consciousness in her eyes. *What will he think? Do I look pretty in this, or dumb?* And he, of course, if he can't be genuinely appreciative, does his best to be tactful. Her feelings are on the line, after all; at the very least, he doesn't want to make trouble.

So there they are: She's excited, presenting herself in a new way, feeling shy, wondering what he's going to think about how she looks; he's in the role of the possible admirer, aware of the effect his words may have on her feelings, waiting for her to come out to him, waiting to see her as he has never seen her before and, thus, metaphorically, to see her with new eyes. She is giving something of herself; he is giving of himself, while each waits in anticipation for the other's giving to shape this simple moment of togetherness. And this anticipation infuses the air with the electricity of a promise, something to come, something to be fulfilled. Now, if this isn't a damned good description of what everybody loves about courtship, I don't know what is. The times I took part in this little ritual as a ritual, I almost immediately found myself feeling again how much I loved this eager, exciting, shy, attractive, new person walking out to show me her stuff and, whether she realized it or not, trusting me enough to open herself up to what I'd have to say about it. Seen from within the circle of the ritual, going shopping with the woman you love has nothing to do with going shopping and everything to do with the woman you love.

Of course, there's the inevitable rift between theory and practice. Some women no more want the man in their life tagging along than the men want to go. Chicken or egg problem, that one. It's a real shame, but the question of who's to blame for the loss of our rituals may be as pointless as blame itself. Obviously, there will always be men who are going to get far more excited watching a couple of two-hundred-fifty-pound linemen in a head-on collision than they will watching their mate twinkle out of a dressing room in black jersey. These men don't know what they're missing any more than do the women who have written them out of these little intimacies, these rituals of love and renewed life that are waiting for us in the most surprising incidentals.

Folding sheets is another example. Rich possibilities there, especially fitted sheets. Somebody's got to lead, somebody follow. It's a great exercise in cooperation that can be loads of fun. You know—she tucks the corner in from the left; you've already started tucking from the right, so you switch, but she sees that you were going the other way so she switches, too. . . . This nothing of a chore reveals our natural tendency to work together, to lead and follow in turn without any need for somebody giving orders. Folding sheets is about community. And if we can naturally, spontaneously look to each other for a hint of how to go on, maybe we can carry this beyond the laundry room. If we could take just a trace of it, say, to the bedroom, or to the tough moments when everything seems to be falling apart, if we could remember that the ritual is always there, that the sacred is always waiting for us to remember . . . who can say what we might discover about each other and ourselves?

Going shopping and folding sheets are just two examples

of how the holy hides in the ordinary, in the washed pocket-handkerchief D. H. Lawrence mentions. Or maybe not. Maybe the mundane details of everyday life are just things to get through so we can go to sleep, wake up, and get through them again. Which is it? This question is really a form of the old saw about the tree falling in the forest with nobody around to hear it. Does it make a sound? Some say it does, because the idea of a tree falling and making no sound is ludicrous to them. Others say it doesn't because, to them, the word *sound* means "something heard," and if there's nobody around to do the hearing, well, then, technically, there's no sound. Don't make the mistake of discounting this as a word game or "mere philosophy." Words start and end wars, and the "merely philosophical" question of the falling tree has great bearing on the idea that the most commonplace activities can be doorways of ritual through which we can reclaim the love and life that we, in our forgetfulness, seem to have misplaced.

What opens these doors? As far as I can tell, two things: willingness and watchfulness. More specifically, the willingness to reach beyond our habits and a watchfulness that pays attention to the details of whatever is before us. This is tougher than it sounds. For one thing, we have to be willing to reexplore territory we've crossed off our list because we've talked ourselves into believing we know it when, in fact, we don't know it at all. Once we've confronted our old resistance, acknowledged it, and made the decision to go ahead and do things differently, we need to slow down because slowing down is the first part of paying attention. The ritual is there. The tree does make a sound. There are an endless number of ways for people to practice being close. But we have to do our part. We have to be there.

My old friend Robert Levine had the best answer I ever

heard to the question of whether or not the tree falling in the forest with nobody around to hear it made a sound. "Sure it made a sound," he said. "Where were you?"

If a dish falls in a restaurant and there's nobody around to hear it, does it make a mess? And who has to clean it up? This may seem like a dumb question, but when you remember finger painting, when you remember that it's all metaphor out here, you discern a not-so-dumb question under the question. The plate is dropping; it's been dropping for generations, as the legacy of dysfunction, negativity, and commitment to fear and pain is handed down. Nobody is dropping the plate anymore; it just keeps falling and breaking, life after life. Who has to clean it up? You do. And I do.

It isn't that hard. Lasting change can begin with a simple decision to open up to a new way of seeing things. A decision to find the ritual. To ask for what you need. To let sadness be sadness instead of twisting it into anger. To celebrate. To allow someone a lie or two when you know that the circumstances are difficult. To practice gratitude even when you can't feel it. To get on a plane and see what things are like somewhere else. To remember a love won and not a love lost, and to move on to love again. To take a deep breath. To take a chance on the truth. To take a chance on yourself.

Face to Face

It takes a man to suffer ignorance and smile,
Be yourself, no matter what they say.

—Sting
"Englishman in New York"

 *A few months ago, Kären went out to dinner with a friend who had run into her old lover, and at the Sunset Grill no less. Kären was furious. As far as she was concerned, the whole place had been defiled. Took her weeks to get over it. Despite the passing of the years, there are some loves that still galvanize us at a glance. We learn to go on with our lives, to work around the emotional black hole created by their absence, but that hole is there nonetheless. And this leaves me wondering if divorce—emotional divorce—is really possible between two people who saw and touched and cared for each other—between wife and husband, brother and sister-in-law, stepparent and stepchild, friend and friend. Kären never sees her former mate, never talks to him—socially, their love is "finished." But if love was there, can it ever be finished? Circumstances, immaturity, poor timing, errors in judgment can disunite the lovers, but*

can love be dismissed, erased, terminated? Can we choose
and unchoose love the way we flick the buttons on the remote
control of a television? Suddenly face to face with my former
wife in a shop or restaurant—this always comes fast, like
tossing ice water at sleep—so many years now after the worst
of it, I still feel a shudder for all that was and, at least physically, is no more. And it seems to me that she feels it, too.
Her eyes avoid, she hurries past a little too quickly—the love
must be given no quarter. Better not.

Time, according to the cliché, is supposed to heal these
wounds, to apply its amnesiac balm, but time has no authority over the heart, and something in us knows and fears this.
In twenty years, two psyches can pick up right where they left
off, in the middle of the last sentence. I've seen it. The sum of
our loves is with us each moment; what the psyche cherishes,
the psyche remembers and, somehow, keeps alive. This is
why we may find ourselves seized by apprehension and a
strange incongruity when an unexpected meeting with a past
partner grabs us by the lapels. And this is why the term "ex-"
is so violent—as though a person could be crossed out, just
like that. Outwardly, in our conduct, we may deny love. But
inwardly, we live amid volatile worlds of reconciliation and
destruction. Their doorways open and close, and there's always both the promise and the danger that any one of them
will draw us through again. If it does, our story will take an
unforeseen, perhaps seemingly miraculous turn, and as always, the transition will be seamless to hindsight. These inner
doors of probability can't be forced; they're opened by an
invisible hand, like the imperceptibly widening vortex of a
flower. Despite all external evidence, we can't take the same
liberties with the heart that we do in our incessant, electronic,
push-button world. We carry with us in some inscrutable
mythic code, the indelible imprint of every love we've known,

*and all our attempts to bury them only succeed in burying
them alive. What happens to love's jettisoned worlds, to those
that never reemerge? What happens to the embrace, the kiss,
the dreams of an amputated life? What becomes of them?*

When I was in the tenth grade, I stood five feet tall and
weighed just over a hundred pounds, so I didn't exactly look
forward to touch football games every Wednesday in physical
education class. Most of the other guys were closer to six feet,
and there were a few knuckle-walkers who thought *touch*
meant *destroy.* Even though I was fast and fairly athletic, my
height and weight ruled out my being taken seriously, especially in such a "man's" game, and when the two captains
took turns choosing up sides, I invariably endured the humiliation of being among the last. You could always tell by who
was chosen after you, just how bad off you were in the peck-
ing order. The guys left after me were the ones with the
Coke-bottle glasses and retainers, and their khaki shorts
hiked up around their chests. So I almost never got to carry
the ball.

On this day that comes to mind, though, something different is going to happen. I can see it now: In a few minutes, the
coach will blow his whistle, signaling the end of the period
and starting a field-wide stampede toward the locker room.
The situation is classic: We're in the last huddle of the game,
one touchdown away from victory, and our quarterback tells
me to go out for a long pass, evidently hoping to baffle the
other team. No matter. I'm going to get my chance.

The ball is snapped; I run out, arcing back as I am supposed to, and the quarterback lets it fly—a beautiful pass that
spirals and floats and finally zeroes right into my hands, raw-
hide slapping. I cut back, then to the left, dodging tacklers

who are, it seems, everywhere. Using all the speed, grit, and hip-swivel I have, I dart through, keep finding open ground, legs hammering. Then, suddenly, I'm in the clear, the goal line just ahead, the yardage closing. I'm running my heart out. Looking back, I see the guys on my team jumping and yelling, fists in the air. Then, feeling like Odysseus must have felt avenging his family at that final, bloody banquet, I cross over into the end zone, ball held high overhead. As I strut back up the field, one of my team members races over to me, gesturing wildly. *"What are you doing?"* he says. *"You ran the wrong way!"*

"I *what?*" I say, looking up and down the field and getting my bearings. It sinks in, and I start arguing, as though my words will lift the field and turn it around, turn my stupid, five-foot, one-hundred-pound life around. I notice members of the enemy camp laughing and clapping their hands together as the coach's whistle shrills and they head for the locker room. Meanwhile, my teammates, standing around in shock, shake their heads and call me different names, most of them involving the words "dumb" and "shit." I wait out on the field until everyone else has left. There isn't much worse than finding out, in what you believed with all your heart was your moment of truth, that somehow, you ran the wrong way.

New scene: Fourteen years later at the University of Florida campus, out on the Plaza of the Americas, where students toss Frisbees, read, sleep, and occasionally even study throughout the day. Gainesville. The whole town looks like it was built in a forest of live oaks. Many of the trees have been here for over a hundred years and are covered with an almost luminous gray hanging moss that makes them look wise and vaguely prehistoric, especially in moonlight. On campus, some trees have been tagged by the forestry department with little aluminum medallions that have numbers on them. It's Valentine's Day, 1979, and I'm about to ask someone to marry me.

I'm nervous as hell. Seven years ago, my first marriage ended, and it's taken me this long to believe in second chances. I've only been seeing this woman for a few weeks; she's young, and I know I'm probably going too fast again, but I want so much to believe in it, to make it work this time. She's sitting beside me, here, under Tree Number 11, and I take this ring from my pocket—we've already picked it out together— to present to her formally. She's an extraordinary woman with long, golden hair and a singing voice that could break the heart of an angel, and her large blue eyes are even wider than usual with anticipation as I open the box and take out the ring. *What are you doing?* She smiles softly. Then, something wonderful happens: Just as I slip the ring onto her finger, exactly then, the carillon bells in Century Tower start playing, an unscheduled performance especially for us, for this moment. The February breeze brushes over us. The ring slides on all the way to where it will stay, I know, forever. Everything fits, feels so uplifting, so right. We hug. We kiss. I am her curly-headed man; she is my diamond-girl. Touchdown.

Five years later, my diamond-girl moved out, and in what seemed like a final, violent flash, our marriage fell apart, leaving me with the same old sense that I had run my heart out in the wrong direction, and that this simply was not possible. Surely, I could talk my way out of it, do more, make it better—I had fought and cared and wanted too hard to wind up walking back to the locker room alone this time. But I couldn't. What was, was. It always is.

In a football game, the situation is simple and straightforward; only the dullest or most preoccupied will manage to misread it and run the wrong way when the right way has everything on it but blinking lights and arrows. Maybe that's why sports are so popular in this jet-lagged hurly-burly of a world. Out on a football field, everything is so clear: It's you against them; there are chalk lines and out-of-bounds markers; there are rules to cover every situation, and you know beforehand how and when they apply. But in the game of love there are no rules because it isn't a game. You either deny what you feel, in which case the demons come streaming out of their graves at night and chase you, or you do your best to follow your heart, sometimes only to find out later that what you thought was your heart was one of your demons having a little sport with your life.

Maybe it's better to say that there are rules, but they're personal, and so they keep changing. Sometimes she's sensitive, open, giving—then something turns, and she's aloof, withdrawn, restless. Today, she feels down and wants your strong arm around her; a day later, somehow that same arm has become patronizing and oppressive. Or, *he* wants the comfort of holding and being held, to lose himself and his worries in long, soft hair and womanly warmth, only to find himself pushing her away when she offers these because he has suddenly become someone else—someone who perceives her offer of herself, of her love, as a threat to his masculine strength and independence, perhaps even as a demand to perform. Or maybe he's just pissed off about something that has nothing to do with her and here she comes, a lovely target. You never really know who you marry because ebbing and flowing in every bride and every groom is an ocean of accumulated losses, unresolved hurts, conditioning, sweeping currents of sanity and insanity, fears, fantasies, longings, expectations, resentments—and you never know what's going to surface next or what it will bring up in *your* ocean. There is, finally, no blame in any of this. What we are is all so *big*. A marriage isn't between two people—that is, the people they think they are—but between two *psyches,* each equally capable of noble devotion and mob rule, of conducting little rituals of selfless love and adoration and also of picking its nose and furtively wiping what it finds there on the bottom of the neighbor's couch. All of these faces *will* emerge from the depths eventually, with no apparent rhyme or reason, and this is what makes the reality of love different from that cotton-candy period of mutual impersonation called courtship. Any two people who have been married for a while and navigated around each other's jagged and falling places, who have looked into the face of the worst in each other and stuck it out together anyway, can tell you that whatever it is that endures on love's roller-coaster ride has nothing to do with never wanting out, or never wondering what it would be like to sleep with somebody else, or never having fantasies of adventure and possibility next to which married life seems hopelessly sedentary and bland. Ironically, this is what makes marriage so exciting and, at the same time, so precarious: We never know who we are because we keep becoming other people—an endless cast of characters who stir and awaken and emerge in full emotional costume and who then walk into the spotlight of the marriage and struggle to find lines they can speak honestly without tearing up the theater. *All* of these characters are assembled at the marriage altar, hidden within the psyches of the two hopefuls—a gang of ghosts, shapeshifters, ancestors, and cartoon characters that probably would scare anybody off: her father, his mother, their grandparents, her sisters, his brother, their former loves and partners, and who knows who else. The whole motley troupe is in on the act of marriage, and this much is certain—none of them, certainly not the angriest or most frightened—is going to simply lie down and go away because somebody is reading some pretty words the couple wrote themselves about forever and such.

All the characters within us, all the people we are, continue to occupy and preoccupy us, to haunt us, to leap out from the wings and look out through our eyes, listen through our ears, talk through our mouth. They will be there at the reception, in bed, in every financial decision, and most of all, in the recurring gut sensations we have about our pledge to be together "till death do us part." There's a chilling phrase if ever there was one, because the work of making peace with this inner rabble, in ourselves and our husband or wife, does seem to take a lifetime. The only way we can divorce *that* is by deciding not to live an inner life at all. And whatever "we" are in the middle of this psychic Woodstock, somehow has to get out of bed, take a shower, go to work, bring up the kids, earn a living, and do the best it can. When you consider all of this, the question is not why so many marriages fail, but how any succeed.

I've asked myself if getting married as quickly as I did was really anything more than just another mistake of passion along the lines of running into the wrong end zone. Had I, once again, with all my heart, simply failed to pay attention? But to what? To whom? Maybe it was to the truth within me, which kept trying to tell me, not that this marriage was wrong, but that a great deal needed attention before *any* marriage could be right. There had been signs, intimations, silent warnings to slow down and face the inner music. But I wasn't willing to listen to those strains, or perhaps I wasn't ready. I insisted on living out a single role, a single image of goodness and romantic devotion. When this papier-mâché mask began to shred and fall away, I finally had to concede my inner complexity. And in this, I began to understand how crazy it had been to attempt to run away from so much of me by pretending to be any one character. Yes, I could read the lines of the sensitive soul, the poet, the romantic; it's a wonderful role, full of lyricism and inspiration and desire. But when played to the exclusion of the rest, as a way of *avoiding* the rest, it becomes tragic, self-effacing, manipulative—the "good boy" who falls in love quickly, admires and adores quickly, and marries quickly, and all the while continuing to feel alone, terrified, fraudulent, lost, inadequate, and angry as hell underneath the yellow roses and lines of verse. How could any idea of a "happy marriage," no matter how passionately pursued, contain all *that* for long?

Since then, I've got a bit better at lighting up the dark corners of my inner stage and letting all the players who hang out there have a go at it from time to time. This has brought some disappointment—our false gods don't die easily—but also a deeply satisfying sense of inner collaboration and renewed vitality. And it has convinced me that there was no mistake in my marriage or in anything else that has happened in my life. Wisdom, as the adage has it, is hindsight, which is another way of saying that things go more or less the way they must, and it makes no sense to label as a mistake what one could not have done otherwise at the time. There are no end zones or lines of scrimmage to guide us in love. We have to learn our own heart as we go, knowing neither what is propelling us nor where it will lead. We may have to hurt ourselves and each other many times along the way before our courage and willingness to admit and be fully who we are make us safe. At some point, we may seize the moment of truth and admit that we don't know, that we've never known what all this running around is about, and if we can only find it in us to live in the nakedness of this not-knowing, eventu-

ally we can stop running. We can come to understand the
territory we've been through, who we were being when we
went through it, and that it was necessary to go through it as
we did.

The part of us that likes to think it knows which way we're
going is like a bad director who projects his biases onto his
actors and tries to fill the stage with half-assed replicas of
himself. A good director recognizes that the talent of a tal-
ented actor is vast, and he deals respectfully with that talent
to bring its power into the focus of his artistic purpose, dancing with what stands before him rather than stacking the
deck with what he already "knows." All our so-called knowing is such a small thing, and our inwardness, so huge—we
can no more *know* the psyche, our own or another's, than
Pecos Bill could rope a twister. Like him, when we try, we
only end up getting carried away. Which means that the only
wrong way to run is from ourselves, from the crazy, rich,
scary, incredible extravagance of our own inwardness.

Psyche *creates* us. We emerge in each moment out of its
prolific depths, in crosscurrents of the many people we have
it in us to be, some wonderful, some terrible, many unpredictable. In the face of these enormous inner forces, the attempt to reduce love or marriage to some game plan, however
sincerely felt, is to miss the point, not only of being in love
with someone but of having a body and emotions. A wedding, like a story, has a beginning, a middle, and an end. But
marriage is not about weddings or even about romance or
being happy together, which are, after all, only more stories.
Love is not a story because it has no beginning, no end. Either
it's all middle or it's just another mask. Marriage *is* about the
daily work of walking willingly into the closets where our
scariest characters, the old demons, have always been waiting, and calling them out. When we've finished yelling,

screaming, crying, talking, holding each other in the middle of the night, shaking, throwing up, name-calling—all the contractions we struggle with in giving birth to ourselves—then we will see what sort of marriage we have. And when we've seen the worst in our husband or wife and understand in our heart not that this is who our partner *really* is, but that this, *too*, is who our partner really is, then we may say we have a marriage. Because then we have faced and appreciated the illogic, the predicament, the free-for-all of the inner life. Then, a deeper love is possible. Michael Ventura describes this well in his candidly written book, *Shadow Dancing in the U.S.A.:*

> . . . sometimes when you are trying to break through the hardened crusts inside you and each other, some dishes and typewriters and furniture might have to go in the bargain . . . . The most odious aspect of the goody-goody, I'm-OK-you're-OK dialogues is their failure to recognize that sometimes you have to scream, slam doors, break furniture, run red lights, and ride the wind even to begin to have the words to describe what is eating you. . . . Anyone afraid of breaking, within and without, is in the wrong marriage. Let it all go. Let the winds blow. Let's see what's left in the morning. . . . And *that* is the "solace of marriage"—a phrase I've heard in several contexts, but am otherwise unable to comprehend. The discovery of what is unbreakable among all that's been broken . . .

Until we're willing to be fully in our body, willing to take what comes up emotionally and pay attention to it, other people can only be our own issues looking back at us. If we try to deny the psyche, she'll turn those we love most into the very actors we are not willing to have walk out on our inner stage. My former wife, for example, had a more or less benign habit of sometimes leaving dresser drawers open and the cap off the toothpaste, which upset me to no end. After she left, the drawers were always conspicuously closed, the cap always screwed tightly in place. At last, I had my way, but instead of satisfaction or a sense of improved order in the household, I felt only an awful finality. In time, I came to realize that the underlying issue for me had nothing to do with dresser drawers or tubes of toothpaste. It had much bigger teeth, and if it hadn't been these things, I would have found some other excuse for acting out what was really gnawing at me. I was already carrying so much in denial, emotionally, that the open drawers, the stray cap, were like little straws breaking the camel's back at every turn. In these details, I heard a recurring voice that whispered, "Things are out of place here, and you are not in control!" This voice had a tone you'd associate with heavy breathing and exorcism, and it set into motion within me tremors I didn't want to feel, since there was indeed something deeply out of place in my psyche, and my control was an impersonation designed to keep the emotional truth at arm's length. I had been running from upsetting sensations of shame, humiliation, betrayal, and grief all my life, running from myself, running the wrong way. Oddly, it was always the littlest things, the props and details of a given moment—the open dresser drawers and uncapped tubes of toothpaste—that most threatened to open the door and let out the terrified, ashamed, and enraged cast of characters I had so long denied an audience.

As we seek to oppress and control our own emotions, so will we seek to oppress and control others, which is why an open dresser drawer can have infuriating power, and how the *denial* of our passions can rob us of our vision. But for those who are willing to let the psyche speak, there are no

mistakes—only times of lesser and greater clarity and cooperation. Living the inner life means loving yourself, marrying
yourself, come hell or high water, forever, with a sacred vow
to sleep with the truth, to make love with the truth, to let the
truth of who you are come in you and fill you with your life.
The language that captures this best is at once sexual and
spiritual, grounded and self-transcendent, streetwise and
ethereal, because *we* are all of these things. Outside, we may
be five feet tall; inside, we straddle worlds. When we can
allow ourselves this much room to be, allowing our loved
ones the same, there's nothing left to prove, nothing to chase,
nothing to run away from. We can begin to choose, out of the
many people within us, which ones we will be.

It comes down to this: If you want to stay sane in love,
forget about keeping score, and marry all of yourself, first.
Then, you can marry all of the person you love. There's a real
glow to that kind of marriage, like the fire in a fireplace—not
the bright flames flickering on the surface, but the coals hidden in the center, where the heat is greatest and lasts long
after you've gone to bed.

I began these notes with some lyrics by Sting; let me end
with some others by Jack Tempchin, whose song, "Peaceful
Easy Feeling," was recorded by the Eagles:

I've got a peaceful, easy feelin',
I know you won't let me down;
'Cause I'm already standin'
On the ground.

This little verse says it well, and it rings true. It doesn't matter
where we think we're going. What matters is to get to where
we are, to stand on the ground under our feet. And all we

have to do to keep from running the wrong way, is stop
running.

*It's late. At the Grill, the chairs are upside down on the
tables, and the plants, caught in the glare of the street lamp
outside, are throwing long, quiescent shadows on the floor.
There are no servers bustling around to keep customers
happy, no lilting fragments of conversation, no flapping
menus. It's as though the whole place has gone to sleep. This
after-hours repose fits the night's meditative stillness, and I
find myself thinking about another place where I used to
meet with friends—the Rathskeller on the University of Florida campus. That was twenty years ago. But the ghost of that
former hangout is here, now, and looking at the sleeping
Grill, I remember how, for years after leaving Gainesville, I'd
wanted to go back, to belong again to the campus life that
had been so fulfilling, the golden age of my political and
intellectual life. But when I finally did go back, Gainesville
wasn't there anymore. In its place was a strangely different
town, a different university with different students, different
teachers, different politics, different priorities. The Gainesville that was an indelible part of my inner life had been
replaced by an imposter. I tried to resurrect the Gainesville I
knew by visiting the places of former riches and rituals—the
restored Hotel Thomas where I got married; Santa Fe Community College, where I taught for five years; the classrooms
in the Arts & Sciences building where I first studied philosophy with Tom Hanna, Jimi Millikan, and other professors;
the old, shingle-roofed apartments where I sat up all night
talking with friends about metaphysics and art and ethics,
where my lovers and I argued with all the puffery and reck-
less passion of headstrong youth, like circus clowns using
oversized clubs to clobber each other, and where, when the*

fighting was over, we'd kissed and held each other until sleep came and brought us another day, another chance to do better. Eventually, I realized that it wasn't just these places that had made my Gainesville what it was, but the time of things that had embraced them.

When I understood that, when I got clear about what the love of that city was and wasn't about, the desire to go back left and never returned. And this says something about the love of anything, or anyone. Inevitably, the outer form changes and, in this sense, is lost. We leave a city. Or get divorced. Or are "asked" to retire. Or receive bad news in the mail. All of these events mark the loss of a love. But through the loss, something of what we have loved stays with us, and makes us more than we would have been without it.

Tomorrow, the Sunset Grill opens again. Somewhere, it always will.

Epilogue: A Tornado Among Men

Early this summer, I planted some flowers in front of my house. Soon, four dozen impatiens, white and orange, were catching the sun and gracing the summer.

Impatiens are delicate flowers, partial to warm weather. They abruptly give up the ghost at the first touch of frost. Every other day, when I water them I marvel at the breakneck pace of their growth. The plants are big and getting bigger, and the blossoms multiply without end.

But I remember the end of last summer, when the crop of impatiens was at its fullness. One evening, I was in front of the house watering my exuberant impatiens. Usually, I have pleasant feelings when I am doing this, but on that particular evening other feelings intruded.

Perhaps it was the nighttime darkness that brought on my unusual mood. Whatever, as I was watering the thick mass of flowers that had swelled

out to the borders of the garden and were enthu-
siastically reaching further, I was struck by a cau-
tionary thought. It was this: "Look at the happy
innocence of these flowers. They have expanded
and multiplied, and they believe they will continue
growing forever. Little do they realize that the killing hand of frost is waiting just around the corner
to destroy them."

That was the thought. Not an unusual thought
but one which bore within it a strange pang. There
was something uncomfortably smug about my at-
titude. I knew something that the flowers did not
know. Here they were, innocently assuming that
life and growth and beauty would go on expanding
forever—not realizing the error of that assumption.

The smugness was my feeling of compassionate
superiority to the plants. They were naively affirm-
ing the eternality of life and growth, and I was
sagely negating it.

When I first thought of the doomed innocence of
the impatiens, there was a genuine feeling of sorrow. I pitied the naiveté of the flowers. I was
knowledgeable; they were not.

But then the realization came that I was not only
smug, I was confused. The killing hand of frost was
not only waiting for the flowers; it was also waiting
for me. In my compassionate superiority, I was
elevating my knowledgeable consciousness above
the exuberant innocence of the plants.

But I, too, was being innocent, because I, too,
would die soon enough.

There was only one difference between the flowers and me: the impatiens affirmed the eternality of

life, and I did not. The impatiens were pure in the way they lived, and I was sullied by a contradiction. My inner sense of the eternal imperative of life was corrupted by a way of thinking that negated that inner sense.

I realized that, all things considered, it was the impatiens who lived life to the fullest, whereas I was living my life hamstrung. It was not I who was superior, but they.

Moreover, I had to ask myself something else: "How do I know you are right about the end of life and they are wrong?" Confessedly, I did not really know. And yet I had smugly affirmed this uncertainty.

Is total affirmation of life and growth the highest good, or is it some kind of sinful ignorance? Should I live awaiting the end that I have envisaged, or should I live expecting only life and only future?

Who is wiser? I, or the impatiens? I think the impatiens are wiser. They assume only what they know and feel. They do not assume something they do not know and feel.

My mother died this last July. She was eighty-five years old. And she was full of life. She had just moved into a home for retired teachers. She was delighted to be there and was eager to make new friends and to begin a new life.

She died one week after entering the retirement home. She died abruptly, while in the midst of expanding her life and growing into new friendships. She died knowing only life.

And so I water my impatiens this summer and into the autumn. And I gaze at their happy inno-

*cence. They are my teachers, just as my mother is
my teacher. And the water sinks down into the soil,
giving life. It is the same soil from which I sprang
and my mother sprang. And it is the same soil that
will receive us both.*

*If I trusted it to give us life at the beginning, I
might just as well trust it to give us life at the end.
In that way, I have joined in a wisdom that tells me
that my mother, my flowers, and I myself are now
together and somehow always will be.*

—Thomas Hanna, "Of the Same Soil"
Somatics/Autumn–Winter 1988–89

On August 6, as I was finishing this manuscript, tragic news arrived in the mail. My former professor, colleague, and friend Tom Hanna had been killed in a car accident in California. The notice read: "Thomas Hanna died at around 5:00 PM on Sunday, July 29, 1990, when he swerved on a country road to avoid another vehicle. His 1966 Ford Bronco slipped on a steep embankment, flipped over and hit a power pole. Tom died instantly."

Stunned, I sat on the couch in a windstorm of disbelief, rage, and emptiness. My heart pounded. I cried out and shook the sheet of paper as though to rearrange the letters into a different message. But they continued to spell out the impossible. I had visited Tom only a few months earlier, in April. We'd kept our friendship active through phone calls and letters, but we hadn't seen each other since university days, and I was struck by his exuberance and vitality; at sixty-one, he stood straight and strong, and seemed to have aged only a few years in twenty. He gave me a quick tour of the Somatics Institute, which he founded in 1975, explaining some of the new approaches he'd devised in the area of functional integration, a system of hands-on, somatic reeducation of the body. Tom's methods had surpassed the pioneering work of his teacher, Moshe Feldenkreis, and were bringing dramatic relief to many clients suffering from disorders that traditional medicine had written off as untreatable.

In a while, we adjourned to an Italian restaurant in the heart of Novato. Tom bantered playfully with the maitre d' and the waiters, charming them, as he could effortlessly, with his warm, resonant southern drawl, aristocratic bearing, and crystal wit. When lunch was ordered, we settled down to discuss matters philosophical, and I was fortunate, for a few hours, to become his student again.

Tom told me that he was working on something called anthropic theory, which held that our development as a species was "programmed" into the Big Bang. With delight, he spun this cosmic tale, describing how helium transformed into hydrogen in the slow, inexorable unfolding of the conditions that would eventually bring forth human consciousness. From the very beginning, we were *meant* to be here, he explained, and to be increasingly free and open, like the expanding universe itself. Freedom and autonomy—the fullest expressions of the individual—were, in Tom's view, the basis of a new metaphysics that would resurrect the American Dream. We are, he felt, that much a part of the great, broadening circle of creation, and were from the start.

What had seized his interest most was the idea that the explosive, expanding impulse set into motion some fifteen billion years ago was still expressing itself in the forward motion of our lives. Everything living has a face, he said, a forward direction. And because of this, because we are the bearers of this cosmic legacy, we have an evolutionary responsibility to make our lives expansive—to follow our passion, our spirit, our most inspired possibilities—to be fully who we are by trusting and acting on what we love. Now, we can do this only by making friends with our body because our body is the site of our passions and the dwelling place of the inner assent that tells us when we're moving forward and when we're not. Because expanding in creative self-expression is a mandate written into the entire cosmos, this moving forward in the increasing embodiment of our most fulfilling possibilities is a fundamental act of friendship and cooperation with the natural order.

As Tom painted this mesmerizing picture of the universe and our ready place in it, he seemed, as always, to be in on some private joke, an endearing quality that showed itself in certain changes in his expression. At times, it appeared that he was about to break right over the crest of a belly laugh; then, he'd back off of that, blinking thoughtfully, his whole expression would soften, and his lips would shift suddenly from a quizzical smile to what looked like sucking on lemon drops. In an intimate and immediate way, more than anything else, this little choreography revealed his intense involvement in the moment. It was the mark of a man living his life, a man in love with his life. As far back as 1970, in the first philosophy course I took with him, he radiated this quietly joyful self-possession, which drew students to him and commanded the respect and admiration of even his starchiest colleagues.

Tom considered himself an educator rather than a therapist or healer, but his work had a strongly clinical component, and during his career as a somaticist, he helped thousands of people to feel better, move better, and regain a level of health and flexibility they hadn't known in years—in some cases, had never known. He believed that sickness is the result of blockage, of the mind/body/spirit holding back, and that, correspondingly, the healing of the human being—whether emotional, spiritual, or physical—comes through learning and taking new steps, and through refusing to stay stuck. If we're unable to move in certain ways because of physical trauma, we can, through somatic retraining, reclaim our impaired ability. And if we're *unwilling* to move—say, to let go of our past or forge our future, our destiny—we put ourselves at the mercy of a bad choice, one that pits us against the current of fifteen billion years of expanding, moving, purposeful energy. Failing to appreciate this, we let ourselves become victims of the past and the future. Denying or overlooking the inner authority altogether, we may end up asking one outer authority after another how to let go, how to get unstuck, how to move ahead with our life. We may as well ask how the universe turned helium into hydrogen into us. There is no "how." It just kept moving forward. So can we.

As the afternoon sun began to decline over Novato, Tom and I finished lunch and talked and laughed while I scrambled to salvage my assumptions about the world in the face of his enormous intellect and irresistible grasp of things. At first I was skeptical, as would be any halfway decent student of philosophy, but the power and passion of his being seemed to corroborate his account. He was a Big Bang all by himself. With the same uneasiness I had felt during the small Bay Area quakes the day before, but more with a rare sense of excitement and discovery, I leaned into the solar winds of his brilliant creativity and warmth and asked him question after question until we had covered all the ground we could for one day, or one life. I wish now that we'd had more time.

Tom dropped me off at the bus stop in Novato, and we shared a few loving words and shook hands—you never know which handshake will be the last. As I got out of the car, he said simply, "It's all the future, now." Riding on the bus back to San Francisco, I remembered a metaphor that Tom had shared with me in a letter a few years earlier, one of the basic metaphors of somatic philosophy: the human being as a tornado. Meteorologic conditions give rise to tornados, which spin and move forward and have "individual" existence, and so it is with us, on a more complex scale. We are somatic entities, formed by fifteen billion years of conditions perfectly programmed to call us forth. Like tornados, we appear to exist independently from our surroundings while in fact, we are and have always been part of them. And we, too, will spin out one day, as Tom said. But for the time being, we're alive, and free to explore how open we can become to our own forces, how far we can go with the gift.

A couple of months later, I flew back out west, to Sonoma's Westerbeike Ranch, for Tom's memorial celebration. And this is exactly what it was—a celebration of a life well lived, a life of enormous courage and contributions, of deep passion and purpose. All of the stories that were shared by friends and family reiterated Thomas Hanna's tremendous spiritual wealth and tireless generosity. The ceremony ended with a bagpiper playing "Amazing Grace" from somewhere in the surrounding woods. Partly because I couldn't see him and partly because bagpipes have a haunting sound anyway, the music took on an eerie, other-worldly quality, as though pulling aside, for a moment, the veil between two worlds—the one that had given us our dear friend and the one that had taken him away. As I was leaving, I picked up a stone to hold onto as a keepsake. Then, remembering Tom's final words to me, I tossed it back into the woods and went on. There is, always it seems, this going on. I hope there was for him, too.